THE
CHALLENGE
OF
RUSSIA

BOOKS BY SHERWOOD EDDY

THE AWAKENING OF INDIA
THE NEW ERA IN ASIA
THE STUDENTS OF ASIA
SUFFERING AND THE WAR
WITH OUR SOLDIERS IN FRANCE
EVERYBODY'S WORLD
FACING THE CRISIS
THE NEW WORLD OF LABOR
NEW CHALLENGES TO FAITH
RELIGION AND SOCIAL JUSTICE
SEX AND YOUTH

THE CHALLENGE OF RUSSIA

BY SHERWOOD EDDY

FARRAR & RINEHART
INCORPORATED
On Murray Hill, NEW YORK

CONTENTS

FOREWORD

Russia is the *terra incognita* of the world today. We make daring and costly efforts in the interests of science to explore the North and South Poles where no man lives, and since Livingstone we have added the Dark Continent to our world of understanding. If we do not know much concerning these areas at least we have no fatal misinformation about them and no attitudes that hinder correct interpretation of any facts we may learn. We have more information about Russia, but we also have more misinformation. It is not too much to say that this one-sixth of our planet is the most misunderstood portion of the globe—and for good reason. The issues concerned in an almost entirely new social order, based upon a new conception of life, affecting the family and the home, morality and religion, liberty and justice, and involving the contrasts of war or peace, love or hate, violence or non-violence, tolerance or persecution, capitalism or communism, all are so vital and bound up with our deepest convictions and our most sacred traditions, that impartial and objective judgment in such cases is difficult or almost impossible.

Yet there is no country that is more important to understand or that is likely more profoundly to affect the rest of the world, whether for good or evil, in the coming years and generations. For Russia has come to stay, at least for a very long time. It is upon us. Whether as a menace, or as a challenge to set our own house in order, or as a vast experiment which may in time work out some values that may be of use to the rest of humanity, we ought to know what is going on in that section of the world. Yet it is almost as difficult as judging Germany in war time. There is misinformation and false propaganda, often well meaning, on both sides.

This book is written in the conviction that Russia constitutes a challenge to America and the world. Though poles apart, both the friends and foes of the Soviet Union will probably object to some of the statements here made, but the manuscript has been submitted for criticism and correction to experts both in Moscow and New York, to learn whether *in point of fact* there were any statements that were untrue or unfair, however much both sides may differ as to their interpretation.

The question is often asked as to how far visitors are able to ascertain the realities of the situation in Russia. It is true that tourist parties visiting the country for the first time, knowing nothing of the language, are partly at the mercy of their guides and interpreters, but our parties have been given every facility for hearing many witnesses on both sides of every question. The writer has made six visits to Russia in connection with his work, twice under the Czarist regime in 1911 and 1912, four times under the present government in 1923, 1926, 1929 and 1930. Year by year we have seen our former acquaintances of the old order both inside and outside the Soviet Union. We have interviewed friends and foes of the present government, foreigners and Russians in every walk of life. We have gone everywhere we wished by night or day with perfect freedom. We have chosen our own interpreters, often taking them from America or finding them among our permanent friends in Russia. We have selected the factories and institutions we wished to inspect, and no suggestion was ever made by the authorities that we should see certain show places or favorable situations. Nowhere have we been accorded greater kindness, courtesy or freedom of movement, or met with more frank, fearless and honest men than many of those in high positions. We have spoken to them and their leaders have replied to us with more rugged and unsparing criticism than in any other country in the world. In no other land do we feel obliged to tell people what we think of them or wherein we differ from them. There is no criticism in this book which we have not frankly and repeatedly stated to the Russian leaders themselves.

With regard to the reliability of Russian statistics, it should be stated that figures and estimates sometimes differ between one department and another, as in many other lands. On the other hand, no other country has to rely so much upon its own statistics, and to stake practically its very life upon them in the supply of the whole population with necessities, and the coordination of every branch of the national economy in production and consumption with the actual needs of the people. We believe that their statistics may be taken, not by any means as infallible, but as on the whole reliable.

The American experts and economists who made an investigation of Russia in 1927 agree with their colleague, Stuart

Chase, when he writes: "Everyone of us leaves Russia with a high opinion of Russian statistical methodology, with a feeling of certainty that the control figures given are as accurate as common sense and hard work can make them, and that the 'two sets of figures' story is an insult to the intelligent mind." [1] After a long residence in Russia, W. H. Chamberlin states that "the Gosplan, in its estimates of industrial development, has shown a tendency to undershoot rather than overshoot the mark."[2]

The writer has endeavored to be objective, impartial and neutral, criticizing freely and unsparingly what he considers to be the serious evils in the soviet system, yet admitting with equal frankness and appreciation any values that may be found in Russia, and any possible suggestions that it may have for other countries, however much he may differ from their principles or practices. We may learn even from a competitor or an opponent with whom we may completely disagree. The reader should remember that the more favorable aspects of Russian life appear in the first chapters, while the more unfavorable facts and a thoroughgoing criticism of the system occur in Chapters IX, X and XIII. The views herein expressed are purely personal and unofficial and in no way involve any organization. In fact, having reached the retirement age, the writer has automatically terminated official connection with the organizations with which he has hitherto been connected.

New York, January 19, 1931.

---

[1] *Soviet Russia in the Second Decade*, p. 36.
[2] *Soviet Russia*, p. 136.

THE
CHALLENGE
OF
RUSSIA

CHAPTER I

THE SIGNIFICANCE OF RUSSIA

For good or for evil, Russia matters profoundly. Up to the time of the great War we had in the world prevailingly one social order. There were advanced and backward nations, but all civilized countries were following a somewhat similar line of evolutionary development. Since the October Revolution in Russia we have on our planet two social orders, antithetic, antipodal, challenging, conflicting, apparently irreconcilable. Here is a new and incalculable fact in modern history.

We can no longer delude ourselves with the comfortable promise of the speedy overthrow of this hostile system. It is becoming fairly obvious that the wish has been father to the thought and that we have been victimized by our own propaganda against Russia, as we were during the war concerning Germany. For a long time we were told every few weeks that the government was about to fall, that men were starving in this "economic vacuum," that they would soon revolt against such hardships and injustice and tyranny. Then suddenly the predicted failure became so ominously successful that Russia was said to be threatening the markets of the world by enormous dumping of grain, timber, pulpwood and other commodities. People are reported as hungrily waiting in bread lines in the cities of Russia while at the same time their government is successfully invading the markets of the world. We shall endeavor to examine the facts in the case.

The significance of the Russian experiment challenges attention. In sheer mass and magnitude Russia is impressive. It is the largest continuous domain under one political jurisdiction. Its 8,144,228 square miles[1] extend across two continents, covering nearly half of Europe and more than a third of Asia. This area is nearly three times the extent of continental United States, and is greater than Canada, the United States and Mexico combined, or about equal to the whole of North America. Its area is four times that of the continent of Europe without Russia, and nearly one-sixth of the habitable land area of the globe.[2] An American living east of Cleveland is nearer to Moscow than many of the eastern inhabitants of the U. S. S. R. Siberia alone, with its vast resources, has an area one and a half times that of the United States and, if peopled with the density of Belgium, would accommodate more than the present population of the entire world.

The population of Russia on October 1, 1930, was approximately 160,000,000.[3] It is now increasing annually

---

[1] Or 21,342,872 square kilometres. A kilometre is .621 miles. *Soviet Union Year Book*, 1930. Of the inhabited portion 81.9 is fit for agriculture, while 24.1 per cent is uninhabited and unsurveyed.

[2] Omitting the uninhabitable portions of the arctic in the 57,510,000 square miles of land.

[3] The population of the present territory of the U. S. S. R. according to the census of 1897 was 106,256,000; according to the census of 1926 it was 147,013,600. *Ten Years of Soviet Power in Figures*, 1917-1927, p. 32.

2.33 per cent, or 3,657,000 a year, while the remainder of Europe combined, with a population of 370,000,000, is increasing less than 3,000,000 a year. This means that the Soviet Union is adding almost exactly 10,000 a day to its population, representing both the largest total and proportion of growth of any country in the world. The average annual birth rate for the last three years has been 42.9 per thousand while the average death rate has been reduced from 28.6 before the war, to 20.7 per thousand at present.[1] All of this is in the face of the most liberal policy on birth control of any government in Europe. The population is as various as it is large, embracing 182 nationalities speaking 149 different languages.

The resources of Russia seem to be as remarkable as its size. Only those of the United States can compare with them. They extend from the arctic of the north to the cotton and silk regions of the south, and from the Pacific on the east to the arms of the Atlantic on the west. Russia is potentially rich in electric and water power, and in the basic resources of coal, iron and oil.[2] Experts estimate that the

---

[1] Statistics furnished by the *Statistical Department of the Gosplan* for 1930. Infant mortality has been reduced from 25 to 19 per cent. The annual rate of increase from 1897 to 1914 was but 1.8 per cent compared to 2.33 per cent at present. Russia, and especially Siberia, seems to be one of the few countries that can increase its population for some generations without reaching its optimum density.

[2] Surveys made for the Czarist government placed the coal reserves of the Empire at 465 billion metric tons. The International Geological Congress estimated the reserves of anthracite in the Donetz basin as the largest in the world; over three times those of Britain and twice those of the United States. *The Economic Organization of the Soviet Union*, Vanguard Press, p. 32.

Soviet Union possesses 2,874 million tons or 35.1 per cent of the oil reserves of the world.[1] Her enormous forests are about equal to those of the United States and Canada combined. Her deposits of manganese, without doubt the most important in the world, are essential to the production of steel, chemicals, and electrical products. Copper, gold and platinum are found in large quantities but have not yet been adequately surveyed.

Russia's 46,434 miles of railway, the second largest system in the world, are increasing at the rate of 1240 miles annually. In arable land the Soviet Union has 1,414,700,000 acres as compared with 878,800,000 in the United States. In cultivated land the United States still stands first with 293,800,000 acres, Russia second with 279,000,000 and India third with 264,900,000 acres.[2] If her present rate of increase is maintained for a decade the U. S. S. R. will be the largest producer and exporter of grain in the world. Typical of the new Russia is the Giant farm, where 500,000 acres of the virgin soil of the prairie are being brought under cultivation with the aid of the most modern machinery in the largest single farm in the world. And it is constantly being enlarged like many of the other state farms.

The imponderable elements in the situation seem to be

---

[1] Russia's reserves of iron ore of 1,647 million tons in the regions thus far surveyed can supply the country for several centuries. In the Urals there are whole mountains of iron ore and the Kursk region, recently investigated, seems to contain more than the balance of Europe's known deposits of 13,000 million tons. *The U. S. S. R. and the World Economy*, p. 139.

[2] *The Economic Organization of the Soviet Union*, p. 34.

more important than the material resources. Russia is a great laboratory of life. Here we have the largest country in the world attempting the boldest experiment in history. Here is a people daring to believe that there are more dynamic motivations than sordid private profit. As Stuart Chase says, the modern Russian "needs no further incentive than the burning zeal to create a new heaven and a new earth which flames in the breast of every good communist. It is something—this flame—that one has to see to appreciate. There is nothing like it anywhere in America, probably nothing like it anywhere in the world today. One would have to go back to Cromwell, or Mahomet, or St. Paul. Will it last? I do not know. All that I can report is that after ten years it still scorches the face of the curious onlooker. No communist in Russia is entitled to draw a salary greater than a bare living of $112 a month, with sometimes housing space provided. At any hour of the day or night a telegram may call him to an industrial post on the Pacific, on the Arctic, in a trackless desert. And he goes." [1]

The experiment in Russia is not only of material but of deep social and psychological significance. Here is a body of men trying to build a new social order in every department of life. Among other things they seek new motivations. From the time of the Manchester school of *laissez faire* economics we have been told that men will only do their best work when they have the opportunity for almost unlimited personal profit, and that the motivation of individual

---

[1] *Soviet Russia in the Second Decade,* p. 49.

self-interest will best work out for the good of all. The actual situation in Russia, however, seems to provide a whole network of incentives which result in similar behavior reactions to the displaced profit motive. It should be remembered also that the motive of profit in western countries always applies to the management and shareholders, not to the mass of wage workers. The manager or worker in a Russian factory responds to no demand from hungry stockholders, but there is the constant pressure of his government and his Party, the social approval of his group, the class consciousness of the whole body of workers not only in Russia but throughout the world.

In the earlier and destructive phases of revolution there is the appeal to moral indignation, the demand for justice, the kindling of flaming hatred against wrong and oppression. There is the appeal to pugnacity, to the fighting instinct of the worker, to throw himself into what appears as a great moral conflict among the "shock troops" on some needy "front." There is the appeal to the will to power, especially to the common man who may be suffering from an inferiority complex. The movement may cater to the worker's vanity, to his sense of self-importance, to the recognition of his worth and personal dignity. Even more powerful is the constant appeal to the heroic, the sacrificial and the ascetic, though always under a new terminology. The dramatic and tragic elements in life are strongly played upon in the profuse propaganda by which workers are roused to action. It seems to give them a feeling of elation and satisfaction to be fighting beside the downtrodden and long-suffering toilers against a whole capitalistic world of bourgeois nations, pictured in their wealth, luxury and greed as exploiting all the weaker peoples of the earth. Instead of personal gain, social acquisitiveness may be made a powerful motivation. A man will sacrifice for his family, perhaps he may for a wider group than we have yet discovered. Social competition, team play and sportsmanship may be as effective and far more socially beneficial than cutthroat, individual competition. Then there is the herd motive, human gregariousness, the appeal to mutual aid and the limitless possibilities of cooperation, which other countries have so little explored. We know what competition can do; but what are the possibilities of cooperation?

When these basic motives are linked to high ethical and idealistic ends, even though they may disavow the orthodox conception of the ethical character of life and repudiate our terminology, when they nevertheless appeal to the highest humanitarian objectives, what psychological possibilities may they not unlock? They do not ask what they consider to be an unnatural and arbitrary, heroic, individual unselfishness, but in a new and healthy environment under a state that plans to abolish all exploitation, there is supposed to be such an identity of interests that each will naturally seek the welfare of all in seeking his own. Furthermore, when inspired by hope, by daring optimism, by the will to live, by the promise of abundant life for all, for full self and social realization, what tasks are too great, what obstacles are too difficult to be overcome? And finally, in spite of a total change of vocabulary, when all these motives are bound up with the religious emotion, though they may loathe the very word, when the fanatical faith, the focused dogmatism, the missionary zeal and heroism of what is in fact, in many aspects, a burning religion, possess and inspire them and send them out to great deeds like the Moslem with his sword of Allah, what may they not hope to accomplish?

It is in this spirit that their Constitution voices their aims: "The abolition of exploitation of men by men, the entire abolition of the division of the people into classes, the suppression of exploiters, the establishment of a socialist society and the victory of socialism in all lands." [1]

Their avowed aim is to abolish all parasitic elements in society, eliminate all secret treaties, free from enslavement millions of laborers in Asia, the colonies and smaller nations, obtain self-determination for oppressed nationalities, provide a complete education free for all and the ultimate equality of all citizens regardless of race and nationality. They aim "to end the domination of capitalism, make war impossible, wipe out state boundaries, transform the whole world into a cooperative commonwealth, and bring about real human brotherhood and freedom." [2] When a country of such magnitude and power becomes harnessed to such an ideal the result is bound to be significant and far-reaching for the world.

The significance of Russia is further enhanced by its uniqueness. Other countries are endeavoring slowly to

---

[1] *Soviet Constitution*, Article 3.
[2] From the Manifesto of the *Third Moscow International*, and the Declaration of Rights of the Third All-Russian Soviet Congress.

change, reform or alter little by little the structure of society. But here is a land whch is building a whole new social order: The plan contemplates, and with many colossal mistakes is actually realizing, a new government, a new industry, collective agriculture, a new education and culture, a new conception of morality and the home, the building of a new Russia and some day of a new world, however little the majority would care to live in such a world. There has never been another movement quite like it, for in many things it is "the first time in history" that such innovations have been attempted.

The experiment is significant for the Russian people. Together with many lapses, delays and partial failures, the casual, lazy, fatalistic Slav seems to be showing signs of change in his very psychology into a titan of energy and practical achievement. It is significant for the nine-tenths of the population who belong to the newly awakened working masses, and to the one-tenth who belong to the once-privileged classes and against whom the system is in open enmity.

The Soviet Union is significant also in the matter of social theory. As between the three main types of capitalism, socialism and communism, the third is now on trial for the first time. This may be a valuable, even though costly, experiment. It may be well to have at least one country free to try new methods. Where they fail, as many do, there may be a lesson for the rest of the world, and when they succeed they may be of benefit to all, as for instance in the still open question as to how far men will respond to higher motives in life.

The significance of Russia, however unwelcome it may be, will be no less if it proves to be a call to others to put their own house in order. If one country overcomes race prejudice, abolishes child labor, insures its unemployed or, even better, eliminates the periodic business cycle of over-production, financial crisis, and unemployment, it is bound to have an effect upon the rest of the world, quite apart from any propaganda of its own or that of noisy communists in other lands. Where their experiments fail they should be known and equally so when they succeed.

The need of understanding Russia is evidenced by the conflicting reports, wild rumors and propaganda in our press today. Very characteristic are the totally contradictory statements in the *New York Times* of two successive days. On November 22, 1930, we read of the reported assassination of Stalin and the mutiny of portions of the army. The Berlin correspondent of the *London Daily Express* telegraphed additional reports which he claimed had evaded the censorship, as follows: "The correspondent said the alleged mutiny of two Red Battalions near Moscow on Wednesday was confirmed by new dispatches today, and added that two other mutinies had occurred, one at Leningrad and another in the navy at Kronstadt, where officers and crew of the gunboat Vorkov were alleged to have been put in irons."

Recent years have produced no more reliable foreign correspondent than Walter Duranty of the *New York Times*. The same night he replied to these reports, as follows:

"Moscow is calm, orderly, dull and unagitated even by rumor, much less by mutinies or assassinations. . . . There is not the faintest evidence of the preposterous alarms that have surpassed all the records of inventiveness for Riga or Berlin 'news sources' and of the credulity of the foreign press and public. . . . Our inventive colleagues abroad, however, seem to forget that unlike the years of 1919 or 1920, when Riga could 'kill' Lenin or Trotsky or have them 'arrest' each other with comfortable security and there would be nothing save an 'official denial' from Moscow, there now are in the Soviet capital a score or more of foreign embassies and legations wholly free from censorship, with the right to send coded telegrams and sealed mail pouches with diplomatic immunity. . . . Many of these diplomats represent countries with scant sympathy for the Soviet and its works. Almost all of them have a personnel familiar with Russian conditions and the language, with friends and fellow-nationals in all strata of Russian life."[1]

It would seem that after thirteen years of such wild reports and eager propaganda usually forwarded from obviously suspicious "sources" of Riga and Berlin, we would have less credulity. Our interest in Russia seems to be guided by emotion rather than by reason. There are reliable sources of information available for those who wish them in the invaluable reports of Walter Duranty to the *New York Times*, W. H. Chamberlin to the *Christian Science Monitor*, Louis Fischer to the *Nation*, and in books like

---

[1] *New York Times*, November 23, 1930.

Maurice Hindus' *Humanity Uprooted*. Others will prefer the almost daily reports of mutinies and revolutions from Riga.

Concerning the significance of the Russian experiment the conservative professor of economics of Duke University, Calvin B. Hoover, after long study in Russia as Fellow of the Social Science Research Council writes: "World opinion remains either uninformed or misinformed about the progress of the greatest economic and social experiment in human history. It is not too much to say that the history of the world for the next fifty years, and perhaps for a much longer period, depends upon the result of events in the Soviet Union during the present year. . . . When the standard of living of the Soviet worker reaches a point where it is somewhat above that of the poorest paid half of the workers of Western Europe, the full significance of the results of the experiment in Soviet Russia will become apparent. . . . Repression of the handful of Communists in the United States, stricter laws against Communist propaganda, police action against Communist agitators at the present time are futile and ill-advised. A recognition of the very real achievements of the Soviet system and a determination to adapt such experimental data as have been developed in Russia to the needs of our own country is all important. . . . If bourgeois civilization is capable of learning from the social and economic experience of Soviet Russia, then the Russian Revolution will have been as real a contribution to human progress as was the French Revolution. . . . Unless the capitalistic order can find ways and means to improve very measurably the standard of living of its lowest classes of laborers, and at the same time to reconcile the economic rivalries between nations, a militant and fanatic Russian Communism will be hammering at the gates of Berlin by the end of the present decade." [1]

We need not be blind to the obvious fact that there is no situation where our judgment is more likely to be affected by the personal equation. Those who want to see the experiment fail, or who are determined, as many are, that a workingmen's government shall not succeed, will find plenty of evidence to their liking. Russia is full of dark facts today, economic, political and social. But they represent only one side of the picture. The poverty and seeming hopelessness at Valley Forge was no evidence of the final failure of the American Revolution. Sons and daughters of a country that was born of revolution should have no necessary antecedent prejudice against another land in far greater travail, however much its methods may differ from our own. Where we find menace we shall oppose it, where we find evils we shall condemn them, where we find values we shall admit them. All are significant and all constitute *The Challenge of Russia*.

---

[1] *Harper's,* October, 1930, p. 598.

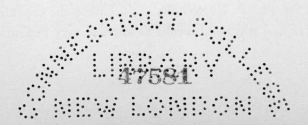

CHAPTER II

WHAT IS COMMUNISM?

Three principal social and economic systems are found in the world today—capitalism, communism and socialism. Capitalism maintains the private ownership of the means of production under a system of open competition and individual initiative for private profit, with a minimum of government interference. Communism, at the other extreme, represents the state ownership and control of all the means of production, distribution and exchange, under a dictatorship of the proletariat, or working class. Socialism, midway between, commonly aims at the gradual socialization of the principal means of production, by consent rather than by compulsion, by constitutional, parliamentary action, through constructive evolutionary processes rather than by sudden, violent revolution. No one of the three systems is found in pure, unmixed form. Capitalism is constantly modified by social control; communism has been forced temporarily to compromise by the capitalistic world, while the process of socialization proceeds but slowly in capitalistic countries.

Let us begin with an examination of communism in theory and in practice as it is found in Soviet Russia today. Communism is at once a philosophy, a method and an organization. As a philosophy it seeks to build a new social order, or classless society, as the result of the abolition of private property and the common ownership of all means of production and distribution. As a method it believes this end can be realized only by a complete social revolution under a dictatorship of the working class.[1] As a party organization it seeks progressively to realize its philosophy by means of a continuing revolution, through a Soviet Government in one country, and through its Comintern, or Third International, by the same revolutionary means in all lands, until its new social order shall be established throughout the world.

There had been utopian dreams of a new social order from the days of Plato's communistic *Republic,* the prophets of Israel, and the early Christian Church in Jerusalem, which had "all things common" in voluntary sharing.[2] From the dawn of history there had been piecemeal revolutions, whether political, economic, social or religious. But never before on a vast scale had there been attempted or realized a complete revolution for the entire transformation of the whole of life. When the largest country in the world, embracing nearly one-sixth of the habitable land area of the globe, attempts the boldest experiment in history, something tremendous is bound to happen, whether for good or evil, or, more probably, for both good and evil. And when such a thing occurs, which is bound to have consequences both wide and deep, we would do well to try to understand it as objectively and dispassionately as we can. Yet we must remember that complete objectivity and freedom from all

---

[1] See the excellent definition in *Communism,* by H. J. Laski, p. 11, to which we are indebted.

[2] Acts 2:44–47, 4:32–35.

antecedent prejudice or passion is difficult in dealing with a situation which, both in theory and practice, roots down into the deepest principles and most pressing problems of human life, involving political, economic, social, religious and moral issues which are vital to us all. When any system touches and proposes radically to change ideas or practices that concern the individual and society, private property, civil liberties, the home and school, church and state, religion and morality, it produces in the minds of most an emotional reaction so strong that it tends to becloud the calm judgment without which we cannot rightly interpret communism, capitalism or any other social theory or practice.

Let us try as impartially as we can to understand just what Russia is trying to do, estimate the present results of the system, and then seek to evaluate their significance for the future.

After a thousand years of despotic autocracy, and some four centuries of Czarism, the revolting intellectual leaders of Russia saw what seemed to them to be the failure of the system of capitalism, imperialism, militarism and recurring wars in the world in general and in Russia in particular. Side by side they saw the few rich landlords and the often landless peasants toiling in bitter poverty. They saw the means of production, private property, profit and power concentrated in the hands of the relatively few, while the masses both in industry and peasant agriculture were dependent upon them with little security of life, often in widespread poverty and want, under needlessly cruel social injustice. The result was a society divided between rich and poor, and a world torn asunder between competing classes, races and nations, a world in chronic, latent strife, which had broken into overt war forty times during the last century and which held the promise of yet more bitter conflict in the century to come. These Russian leaders believed that the root evil of the whole system was private property, appealing to the greed of selfish individualism and mutually antagonistic classes, resulting inevitably in class conflict, as well as national and imperialistic wars.

In place of this system they conceived another, in complete antithesis to the old order, differing in aim, in method and in motivation. Their *aim* was the abolition of all exploitation of man by man through the private ownership and control of the means of livelihood, and the substitution of the good life for all, upon an equal basis of social justice. Their *method* was the complete overthrow of the old, unjust social order by the only means that they believed was left to them, as every other had been tried and had seemed to fail—the same that had been used by the colonists in America in 1776, and by the French against the Bourbon autocracy in 1789, the method of revolution. The instrument was the only class that had not failed them and which they believed they could trust, the long exploited and suffering workers. Their *motive* was to be, not private profit for selfish, individual gain, but public service for the common good.

But could this vast transition be affected in a world of greed, of strife and injustice so deep-rooted that it seemed ingrained in human nature itself? They believed that it could. And it was their daring innovation, in almost unprecedented faith in human nature, that, not in the dreams of Plato's *Republic*, Bacon's *Atlantis* or Thomas More's *Utopia*, nor in a small, homogeneous community of the Greek city-state or the early church, but in the largest and most diverse country in the world this experiment should be actually undertaken. Russia is unique in that for the first time in history on a vast scale this boldest experiment was tried under what seemed impossible circumstances, in the face of titanic obstacles, in what seemed the least favorable land, and against the opposition of almost the entire world.

Let us note, however, that, relative to the rest of the world under another social order, an essential and inescapable contradiction lies at the very center and heart of the whole system. The communist philosophy seeks a new order, a classless society of unbroken brotherhood, what the Hebrew prophets would have called a reign of righteousness on earth. But these high humanitarian ends it seeks by the means of a class dictatorship and by all necessary use of force. It abandons the method of consent, as the costly and priceless acquirement of slow centuries of political progress, for the more primitive method of coercion. It turns back from the achievement of law to primal force, from the disciplines of liberty to earlier and easier autocracy. It seeks justice if necessary by violence, whether supported by a majority or a minority. Once this precedent of force is established, it may easily, or possibly inevitably, become a habit. Dictatorships tend to perpetuate themselves and to require a growing rather than a lessening compulsion. Here then at the center and source we find the cause which makes Russia not only the land of limitless possibilities but also of "limitless contradictions" as well. These contradictions permeate almost the entire system—*high humanitarian aims realized if necessary by ruthless means.*

Hence we find in Russia the most glaring contrasts and the most unbelievable contradictions, the most audacious plans and achievements of social welfare for the masses, side by side with the most unfeeling infliction of pain, privation, punishment or persecution upon individuals; the most generous sharing of every privilege with their class comrades, the most ruthless treatment of those whom they count their class enemies. This is due first of all to the Marxian theory of revolution, but also in part to the character of the Russian people. Russia had never known true liberty. She has always been governed by an autocracy, whether Czarist or communist. Liberty and democracy were both lightly counted as mere "bourgeois prejudices." There is moreover a strain not only of rugged realism but often of cruelty which runs through all Russian and Tartar blood. The repeated massacres of the Jews fomented by the church and state under the old order find their counterpart in the colder and more calculated cruelty of the new regime toward their class enemies, though strangely enough they seem for the most part quite unaware of this cruelty.

To answer intelligently the question What is communism? we must remind ourselves of its theory as propounded by Marx and of the stages through which it has already passed in Russia. The theory is all the more important when we remember that no other philosophy of life was ever so quickly and completely embodied in a new social order upon such a vast scale.

Karl Marx (1818-1883), the son of a Jewish jurist and grandson of a German Rabbi, received from his teacher, Hegel, his dialectic method which held that change takes place through the struggle of antagonistic elements, resolved into a higher synthesis. According to Professor Laski, his social system may be resolved into a philosophy of history, a theory of social development, a tactic for its accomplishment and an economic theory upon which to base the justification for this transformation.[1]

His philosophy is based upon the materialist or economic interpretation of history, which holds that the *principal* influence which shapes the progress of society is the system of economic production, or the way men make their living. This chiefly molds their political, social, intellectual, religious and moral relationships.[2] Therefore, he maintains that those who control the means of production largely dominate the life of the dependent masses. Society becomes divided into possessors and the dispossessed, and the natural and inevitable antagonism between the two creates the class war which becomes the chief instrument of social development. The tactic for its accomplishment is found in the development of the trade unions which are the product of the class

---

[1] See *Communism* by H. J. Laski, p. 25; and a *History of Socialist Thought,* by H. W. Laidler, p. 199.

[2] "The mode of production in material life determines the general character of the social, political and spiritual processes of life." Marx, *Critique of Political Economy,* p. 11.

struggle. Marx maintains that history shows that the possessing class, whether under slavery, feudalism, or capitalism, will never voluntarily surrender its power; therefore,
the organized workers must seize the state and establish a
temporary dictatorship as the only possible means of accom-
plishing the transition from a capitalist to a communist
society.

Marx then develops his economic theory on which to base
his justification for this necessity. He accepts the classic
economic theory of his day from Ricardo that value is the
product of labor. He tries to show that as labor produces
more than it receives, it is robbed by the capitalist of the full
value it produces and receives only the lowest market price,
while all the surplus goes to the employer.

His labor theory of value and of surplus value are not
deemed adequate in scientific theory today, apart from his
own followers, but the character and results of his work are
not radically affected by this fact. Marx was a great sociol-
ogist rather than a modern scientific economist. Like Newton or Darwin in their fields, Marx was a pathfinder in his.
The theories of each of these pioneers must be corrected by
more recent scientific experiment, but few men have influ-
enced the course of history in succeeding generations more
than Marx.

Marxian theories found their classic expression in the
Communist Manifesto issued by Marx and Engels in the
revolutionary year, 1848. He maintains that the growing
poverty of the workers, and the increasing concentration of

capital in the hands of a few hasten the class war and secure the "death-knell of capitalist private property."[1]

Marx conceived his system as an almost complete philosophy of life both as a theory and a plan of action worked out in detail in his embittered poverty, chiefly during his thirty years of exile in London. It was the part of Lenin and the majority of his cabinet who had spent twenty years in prison, in poverty and exile, concretely to apply and adapt this theory to the life of an entire nation in Russia. The whole movement became practically the materialistic religion of the embittered and aroused working class. It took the place of the solace of an other-worldly religion which Marx maintained had become the drug or soporific opiate of the people. Of this new substitute for the old religion the writings of Marx became, as it were, the Old Testament, the thirty volumes of Lenin became the canonical New Testament now in process of translation into thirty-five languages by the Third International, while Stalin is now writing in deeds rather than in words the orthodox epistles of the new faith.

The principles and policies of Marx and Lenin have given a kind of classic basis and orthodox norm to the new movement, but one of its most notable characteristics has been its continuous change and its quick and constant adapta-

---

[1] Marx writes: "Concentration of the means of production and socialization of labor finally reach a point where they become incompatible with their capitalist integument. Their integument is burst asunder . . . The expropriators are expropriated." He was a Jewish prophet of social righteousness who roused the workers to a sense of their wrongs and united them into a militant body by giving them an artificially simplified practical philosophy and a plan of campaign to win their freedom.

tion to the circumstances of a rapidly altering environment. Probably no government in the world in the last dozen years has made so many colossal experiments or so many mistakes; none has confessed to so many failures and defects; none has been so quick to adapt itself to changing conditions. To understand communism today we must not only constantly remember its social philosophy as worked out by Marx, but the stages through which it has passed or which it is destined to enter:

1. WAR COMMUNISM, 1917-1921

Following a thousand years of autocratic despotism, the intolerable government of Russia was overthrown after well-nigh a century of revolutionary struggle, dating from the December revolt of 1825. A blind bureaucracy had opposed all reforms, suppressed or crushed its conquered nationalities, minorities and sects, dissolved or treated with contempt its Duma, outlawed trade unions and put down peasant revolts and industrial strikes with bloodshed. Two hundred thousand landlords owned more than a quarter of all the arable land of Russia while sixteen million peasant households lived in miserable poverty. Over 60 per cent of the people were left in illiteracy. The spy and police system both in state and church had developed into "a vast secret society which permeated and poisoned the whole of Russian social life."

In the World War Russia suffered more than any other great nation. Of over 15,000,000 called to the colors, 1,700,000 fell among the battle dead, and a total of over

3,000,000 died of wounds, disease, neglect and starvation. Betrayed by their corrupt leaders, left often without munitions and supplies, the morale of the troops at the front was finally broken, and the hungry mobs in Petrograd rose in bread riots, only to be shot down by the troops. The soldiers poured back from the front demanding bread, land and peace. On March 12, 1917, the first revolution broke out in Russia, and the Czar Nicholas II abdicated. A provisional Government under Prince Lvoff was set up by the Duma, followed by a new cabinet under Alexander Kerensky. Kerensky's oratory could not stay the retreating troops, and Russia was drifting rapidly into chaos. Only one party knew just what it wanted and had the clarity and courage to give the disillusioned masses the three things they demanded—bread, land and peace. That was the Bolshevik or majority wing of the Marxian Social Democratic Labor Party.

On November 7, 1917, the second, or Russian Workers' Revolution occurred, when by what was at first an almost bloodless struggle, the Petrograd Soviet seized the government authority and handed it over next day to the All-Russian Congress of Soviets.[1]

For three years the government tried to bring order out of chaos. Workers took over factories without the consent of the central government and made a dismal failure in their inexperienced and undisciplined ignorance. The government was forced to centralize and assume authority faster

---

[1] According to their calendar it is called the "October Revolution."

than it wished, and during this period of military communism the state tried to organize almost the whole life of the people on a communal basis. This bold experiment was tried and it failed. For three years private shops were closed and buying and selling often gave place to barter. The disorganized factories could not produce the necessary supplies for the hungry population, and industrial production fell to some seventeen per cent of its pre-war maximum.

The peasants' entire surplus of grain was forcibly taken by the state to support the army and industrial workers. A flood of paper money debased the now worthless currency. The country was exhausted by war and impoverished by a world blockade. It suffered from intervention and invasion and had to fight in turn against the Germans and Austrians, the British, French, Japanese, Czecho-Slovaks, Poles, Finns, Greeks and Roumanians. Even an American army invaded their territory. The white armies of Deniken, Kolchak, Yudenich, Semenoff, Wrangel, Petlura and the Cossacks were not only fighting but often perpetrating atrocities upon the inhabitants, so that at one time the Soviets were engaged on a dozen fronts. After six years of strife following 1914, exhausted by both war and revolution, swept by terrible epidemics and the famine of 1921 during which some three millions perished, Russia finally collapsed in sheer exhaustion. Peasant uprisings began to increase and the area cultivated was reduced to half what it had been before the war. The peasant uprising in the province of Tambov and the revolt in the fortress of Cronstadt showed the handwriting on the wall. War communism in the midst of chaos and with the world against them had failed. Lenin saw their failure, confessed it, and threw his entire weight into a right about face and call for a temporary strategic retreat. Not for a moment were the principles of future program abandoned but they were forced to compromise for the time being in the state capitalism of the New Economic Policy.[1]

2. THE NEW ECONOMIC POLICY, 1921-1927

This was a temporary compromise between state capitalism and private capitalism. The state ran the principal industries for profit, while it permitted private trading and industrial enterprise side by side in open competition. This was the period of peaceful economic rehabilitation and the slow and painful restoration of depleted industry and agriculture to their pre-war productivity. The New Economic Policy included a definite food tax in place of the requisition of the peasants' surplus grain, freedom of trade within Russia, the revival of small capitalist production and of banks and shops on a profit-making basis, the concentration of state

---

[1] In *Izvestia*, August 11, 1921, Lenin frankly said: "We can only continue to exist by making an appeal to the peasants . . . The role of the proletariat in such a situation is to supervise and guide these small farmers in their transition to socialized, collective, communal labor . . . Ten years at least, and, in view of our present ruin, probably more will be required for this transition . . . We must decide which of two policies we shall choose. Either we forbid absolutely every private exchange of goods or we take the trouble to make it a state capitalism . . . State capitalism is a step forward toward the destruction of the small bourgeois attitude . . . The kernel of the situation is that one must find a means of directing the evolution of capitalism in the bed of state capitalism so as to insure the transition of state capitalism into Socialism."

control to the more important nationalized industries, the institution of a State Bank and the encouragement of the Cooperative Societies which had been temporarily absorbed by the state. Although state capitalism and private capitalism were allowed to exist side by side and to compete, the government threw its whole weight on the side of the state industries which steadily waxed while private trade waned until today not only the whole of foreign trade, which has always been a government monopoly, but almost all industrial production, as well as internal wholesale and retail trade, is in the hands of government or the Cooperative Societies. Once industry and agriculture were reestablished, the government was ready for the present advance which is a return to Lenin's original policy of the complete socialization and mechanization of industry and agriculture, the government development of electric power and an advance from state and private capitalism toward their permanent policy of state socialism.

3. STALIN'S DRIVE FOR SOCIALIZATION, 1928-1933.

This marks the third stage of the revolution in the reconstruction of the country's productive life on a new technical basis. More than a decade ago the revolution began in the cities, in government and industry; at last it has reached the villages. At first the Soviet Government endeavored to socialize the three million workers in industry, today it plans to embrace the more than one hundred and thirty million of the peasant population engaged in agriculture.

The plans for this great advance are almost as daring and far-reaching as those inaugurated by Lenin in 1917. Probably no other country ever deliberately launched such an ambitious plan for its economic development within a period of five years. It is difficult to grasp the magnitude of the task. The average size farm among the 26 million peasant holdings in 1928 was but twelve acres. Productivity was low and methods antiquated. The conservative peasant plowed with his iron-shod pointed stick, reaped with his sickle and threshed with his hand flail. The casual Slav was lazy and unbusinesslike. Industry was backward and poorly equipped. The average worker in Russia was producing 164 tons of coal while the American miner produced 715 tons. While the Russian worker produced 218 tons of pig iron, the American turned out 1270 tons, or six times as much.[1] The same was true in cotton spinning, beet sugar and most other industries. With backward agriculture and industry, the undisciplined Slavic temperament, without adequate capital or foreign loans and with wellnigh the whole world against them, how could Russia industrialize, socialize, mechanize and rationalize her entire economy within five years? Yet this is the titanic task to which she has set herself.

The *Gosplan* or State Planning Commission, following out Lenin's original scheme for widespread electrification under a "planned economy," prepared a preliminary draft of the scheme, which when revised and corrected was to run

---

[1] Stalin's address at the opening of the Sixteenth Congress of the Communist Party, *Izvestia*, July 11, 1930.

from October 1, 1928, to September 30, 1933. Every branch of national economy was covered in industry, agriculture, transportation, building, etc., in the most audacious economic program ever conceived, and it was to be applied in detail, with annually revised "control figures." The plan was worked out and charted for each industry and each factory so that every year the exact measure of its success or failure could be verified, and the workers of each factory or collective farm could be roused to enthusiasm to reach their goal, or beat their record, or those of surrounding or competing institutions.

When Stalin faced the economic problem of Russia in 1927 over 95 per cent of the land was retained by individual peasants. Of these 3.3 were rich peasants, or *kulaks*, 66.4 were graded as "middle" peasants, and 30.3 per cent poor peasants.[1]

Broadly, one of two policies had to be adopted. The government might encourage production on small scale individual farms and run the risk of facing a future individualistic and capitalistic peasant class of 130 millions, or over 80 per cent of the population, completely out of harmony with Soviet social aims; or, at the risk of killing the goose that laid the golden egg for Russia's export of grain, it might rapidly socialize agriculture as it had already socialized industry. It chose the latter course. Trotzky had proposed a solution of the agrarian crisis by intensive collectivization and the suppression of the rich peasants. The Communist

---

[1] *Russia's Agrarian Problem,* Foreign Policy Association, p. 191; *Piateletnii Plan,* Vol. II, Part I, p. 271.

party rejected the solution as at that time premature. But early in 1930 under Stalin's leadership the government launched a movement for "complete collectivization" and the "liquidation or abolition of the *kulaks as a class.*"

The word *kulak,* literally *fist,* means an exploiter; one who gains not by his own labor, but by hiring and exploiting the labor of others, loaning money, buying crops and renting machinery, thus endeavoring to monopolize the profit that all should share. Many such had acquired the land of poorer peasants and had enriched themselves at their expense. But there were many who by superior intelligence, initiative and effort were merely prosperous. The whole system has little regard for the individual and many of these as well as the exploiters had their property confiscated and were despoiled or deported. Over-zealous local authorities sometimes ruthlessly carried out the program of almost forcible collectivization. This produced the indignant opposition not only of the rich but of many of the middle peasants and occasioned not only violent protest but almost civil war in some districts. Stalin in March, 1930, called a halt to this over-rapid and at times forcible collectivization. Nevertheless the movement is so bold and sweeping that it marks broadly, for the first time in history, a turning on a vast scale from a capitalist to a socialist system in agriculture. Whether it be wise or unwise, what other country ever contemplated the practical suppression of all exploiters?

The five year program had counted upon some 22 per cent of the peasant population being collectivized. But by June, 1930, already 24.5 per cent, some six million households, or one quarter of the entire peasant population, had been gathered into collectives, while of the spring sowing for 1930, 37 per cent was in collective as opposed to individual farms. Thus the "socialized sector" is being steadily increased at the expense of the private sector.

It is not for a moment to be supposed that this vast transition and metamorphosis of the whole of government, industry, agriculture, and even of the very psychology of the Russian peasant, is being accomplished without great hardship and suffering to multitudes, nor without privation and injustice to many. The government has staked everything on this five-year program to increase the production of agriculture by more than one-half and of heavy industry more than threefold. It has "liquidated" or wiped out the rich and prosperous peasant, with the loss of income from his taxes and his surplus grain for export, and taxed the prosperous Nep man, trader and profiteer almost out of existence. It has honestly sought, not the greatest amount of profit or comfort for the masses at the moment, but, from their point of view, a socially right system which will yield the greatest good to the greatest number in the long run.

To accomplish this program at all costs it must have the necessary machinery, the raw materials and the experts from abroad to enable it to carry out the whole project. But all this must be paid for and their credit maintained. Since there is little gold in the country, and since they are unwilling to touch the priceless jewels and art treasures of the old regime, they can only pay by the export of goods and grain. Cutting down to the bone and denying themselves all luxuries they calculate just how much they require to feed and clothe their population. This ration would be barely sufficient with an ideal system of transportation and exchange. But nothing is ideal, especially in Russia, old or new. With faulty exchange and distribution the pinch is felt by certain portions of the population, and strangely, nowhere more than in Moscow, the most overcrowded city in the world. They are straining every nerve to treble their "heavy industry," i.e. all that is needed for future production in electric power, coal, iron, steel, oil, machinery, etc. They do not care half so much about the light industry for the comfort of the people, including clothing, shoes, and a hundred articles that would be considered the luxuries, necessities and even the decencies of life in western countries. But to their honor be it said, they count no price too great, no sacrifice too severe to enable them to accomplish their objective. Through the press, by speeches, parades, meetings and celebrations, by their own skilful and effective motion picture films, which are not commercialized for the profit of a few, but always made to serve a great social end, through the Party, the trade unions and the youth movement the effort is made, and with amazing success, to enthuse labor and to keep them at concert pitch in a kind of sustained wartime heroism and spirit of sacrifice. By social competition, pitting themselves against themselves, against the goals of the plan, factory against factory, plying them with many motives that may be as effective as private profit, they maintain this terrific national drive. And this at the cost of the inconvenience or privation of the majority, yet sustained by the enthusiasm of labor. At their powerful motion pictures you see the audience moved not by wild-west adventure or love romance but by the triumph of tractors, giant farms, factories and railways. They are thrilled because these things are their own.

Bread is relatively plentiful and cheap at the government stores, but they are short of almost all other supplies of foodstuffs and clothing. The result is long lines or queues of patiently waiting people for the daily, insufficient supply of most necessities. They are short of meats, fats, butter, eggs, milk, sugar—almost everything. But are they downhearted? No more than the British army driven back in retreat before the Germans. No more than the American colonists at Valley Forge. Russia in fact is at her Valley Forge even now. She has been there ever since 1917 and she will know the present privation for several years yet to come. The hardy peasant today roars his complaints, which he never dared to voice against the Czarist terror. But he would fight again, and even more fiercely, on behalf of the present government if another fatal intervention or invasion were ever attempted. With all the hardships and failures and often hating the changes and improvements he is forced to make, he knows that he is better off than he ever was before. Moreover, he is the most long-suffering peasant that ever was, outside the fatalistic followers of Islam. It took over a hundred years to rouse him even to his first Revolution.

The government whose downfall was confidently prophesied almost every two weeks for a long time after it was founded over thirteen years ago was never so strong as it is today. While it is to be hoped that its evils may be corrected, with those of other lands as well, economically it is succeeding, and will succeed, in the judgment of a majority of the economic experts, at least of those who are not determined that a workingman's government shall not and must not succeed.

The man who is directing this vast transition is Joseph V. Stalin. Like Marx and Lenin before him he had long suffered for his convictions. After the age of nineteen he was exiled to Siberia six times by the government of the Czars. Five times he escaped. Finally he was deported in 1913 and remained in exile until the first Revolution. Before his death Lenin had pronounced Stalin "crude and narrow-minded." Yet he succeeded in stopping Trotzky's mouth, expelling his three rivals on the left and subjugating the three on the right of the Party. He is not, however, a one-man autocratic dictator. He and Mussolini are each a parliament in themselves. They hear the aspirations and demands of the multitude. They believe they know in advance just what the people need, just how much they will bear, and what policies will succeed. Stalin leads but in such a way as to keep the backing of the majority in each executive committee and legislative body. It is better for the prosperity of Russia and the peace of the rest of the world that Stalin should lead, rather than the far more brilliant and dangerous Trotzky. Stalin rules, not as did Lenin by a great personality, but by his sagacity, his honesty, his rugged courage, his indomitable will and titanic energy, as well as by force. A mountaineer peasant, a somewhat ruth-

less Georgian Asiatic, Stalin drives his machine like a giant
tractor or steam roller. He pushes irresistibly forward in
the great process of socialization, collectivization, rationali-
zation. When too many are crushed by the great machine
and the outcry of those who suffer becomes too great, he puts
on the brakes or even backs up for a little, only to drive forward again in the irresistible process of socialization which
he wholeheartedly believes will mean so much for the final
well-being of the Russian masses and of the world.

In his interview with Walter Duranty of the *New York
Times*[1] Stalin, as a man of deeds rather than words, was true
to his own theory and practice when he said: "Propaganda
doesn't do anything. Constitutions and systems are changed
by natural causes not by talk or books. In the old days the
Czars blamed the French or German socialists for importing
socialism into Russia, forgetting that the conditions of life
and not the socialist propaganda determine the course of
events. Now I suppose they are making the same mistake
in the United States when they say we are re-exporting socialism to Europe." Like Marx and Lenin before him Stalin
will live and die a poor man. With prodigious toil and
through much hardship he seeks the uplift of the long-ex-
ploited masses. He may fail or he may succeed. But if,
after ten thousand years of competitive strife, of endless
wars and the scramble for private gain, one vast land could
really be socialized and learn the life of cooperative sharing,
its possible significance for human life can hardly be imagined. Its ideal ends may be more important than its ruthless

---

[1] Reported December 1, 1930.

methods. Its methods may be modified, for the Russians are great realists, but its ends will doubtless endure.

We have briefly traced the three stages in the development of the movement in Russia through war communism, the New Economic Policy, and the present drive toward socialization. According to their theory two stages yet remain. The present compromise, or mixture of state capitalism and private capitalism, must give place to thoroughgoing state socialism. Then the state will own and control everything except the life and limited personal property of its citizens. But this is not the final stage. State socialism is to give place, according to both Marx and Lenin, to pure communism. Then the state will no longer be needed to make and enforce laws or compel obedience, but it will "wither away" and cease to be. Communism, which Lenin often used interchangeably with socialism, is simply completed socialism. Lenin writes: "Only in communist society . . . when there are no longer any classes . . . only then does the state disappear, and can one speak of freedom. . . . Only then will democracy itself begin to wither away by virtue of the simple fact that, freed from capitalist slavery . . . people will gradually become accustomed to the observance of the elementary rules of social life. They will become accustomed to their observance without force, without constraint, without subjection, without the special apparatus of compulsion which is called the State."[1]

In the glowing future new generations trained from their youth up in socialized cooperative habits will be expected to

---

[1] *The State and Revolution.* See also *Liberty Under the Soviets,* p. 20.

do right because they desire to do so. A reconditioned and re-educated humanity will build a new earth, if not a new heaven. In their dream industrial workers will eagerly share with the peasants, and the farmers with the city workers. They expect to achieve this classless society where man shall no longer exploit his fellow man, but will rejoice to share all with all. The unshaken faith of the communist in this miraculous future is not wholly unlike the millenial faith of the literalist, fundamentalist religionist. Both have the advantage, as well as the disadvantage of the sharp cutting edge of a narrow dogmatism. In the meantime with boundless energy the communist seeks to make his dreams come true by translating them into action and embodying them in organization. For good or evil he is making history faster than he can write it.

We have tried to answer the question What is communism?, tracing it from its Marxian theory and philosophy, through its practice as it was embodied by Lenin and Stalin in the Russian Soviet State, and through the successive stages of its development. Reserving until later our evaluation of the system and the criticisms and indictments which we must bring against it, let us now inquire as to the significance of the Russian experiment, and how it is working in agriculture, in industry, in the trade unions of the labor movement, in the cooperative organizations, in its cultural activities, in the spheres of education, art, religion and morality, as well as in its political organizations of the Communist Party, the Soviet Government and the Third International.

CHAPTER III

The most important issue in Russia today is the five year plan which aims at the trebling of production in heavy industry and the collectivization of agriculture. With 82 per cent of its population rural, much of Russia, as one vast, almost unbroken, alluvial plain, must stand or fall by its agriculture. The present agrarian revolution may have a significance and magnitude second only to the great industrial revolution of the eighteenth century. It is probably the most thoroughgoing agrarian upheaval in history. The significance of the present movement can only be understood in the light of the past history of the country.

More than two centuries of Tartar rule had isolated Russia and left it the most backward country in Europe. It had helped to fasten autocracy and serfdom upon the country; it had left the masses in bondage and the officials in habits of oriental corruption. The conquests achieved by Ivan the Terrible and Peter the Great, both of whom had murdered their own sons, had crushed a multitude of non-Russian peoples and peasantry. In 1675 the serfs were reduced well-nigh to slavery and could be sold apart from the land. The landowners held practically the power of life and death over the serfs who were mercilessly whipped into submission. The vast peasant uprisings of 1667 and 1773, with their

40

massacres of landlords and officials, were only typical of a
long line of revolts caused by desperation and poverty. As
late as 1861 Alexander II liberated nearly eleven million
serfs owned by the Czar or the state, and an equal number
belonging to private owners.

The peasants were allotted the worst land, for which they
were forced to pay more than it was worth, and in addition
were saddled with the heaviest burden of taxes.[1] The land
for the most part belonged not to individual peasants, but
to the village community as a whole, called the mir, which
periodically redistributed it in small widely separated strips,
in a hopeless fragmentation of land under a system that
provided no incentive for improvement and was fatal to
progressive farming. By the time of the Revolution in
1917, 200,000 landlords owned over a quarter of the arable
land in European Russia and were prevailingly looked upon
with hatred by the 16,000,000 land-hungry peasant households. Over 60 per cent of the latter were illiterate, dwelling
miserably in huts, in villages without paving, water, sewers
or lights, with a standard of living estimated at about 25 per
cent of that of the average American farmer. They were
intensely individualistic, conservative, averse to change and
to modern methods. Even the rich peasants had no knowledge of agricultural machinery and the poor could not make
a living.

A new peasantry is now arising in the present volcanic

---

[1] Of $104,000,000 collected in taxes in a year by Alexander II all but
$6,500,000 came from the peasants. See Chamberlin's *Soviet Russia*,
pp. 14–26, to which we are indebted here.

agrarian upheaval. The two million Russian soldiers captured by the Germans during the World War brought back with them new ideas born of German farming methods. The Revolution that followed, the introduction of modern methods and mechanized agriculture on the state and collective farms all about them, the new school, the new spirit in the town meeting, participation in local government, the motion picture, the innovations and reforms of the youth movement led by their own children—all have produced a storm of new ideas which have burst upon the peasants like a cyclone.

By one of its earliest decrees, November 7, 1917, the Soviet government nationalized the soil and forever abolished private property in land.[1] The peasants who took possession directly from the old landlords regarded the land as their own. The increasing fractioning of land, the antiquated methods of farming and the capitalistic and exploiting tendencies developed by the concessions of the new economic policy produced an unsatisfactory yield with no export of grain, which had been the chief asset of the old régime.

Lenin was convinced that the collective cultivation of land on large farms, with the introduction of machinery and

---

[1] All land was held in trust by the state for all the people, under a system of perpetual leasehold. Individuals received the use of the land provided they farmed it with their own labor. The hiring of labor was prohibited. The October Revolution gave possession of 370,650,000 acres of land to the peasants, who now hold 96.5 of the arable land together with 32,123,000 acres of forest land. Taxation has been reduced to an average of about $2.00 per person a year.

modern methods of industrialization, offered at once the only economic and social solution of the stubborn peasant problem. But not until a decade later under Stalin's leadership was Russia ready to attempt this bold advance. The Fifteenth Congress of the Communist Party, in December 1927, approved of the policy of Stalin for a "gradual transition" to large scale production. The *kulaks,* seeing that collectivization meant the end of their power, naturally opposed the movement, even by acts of murder and arson, with the result of "class war" in many villages. In 1928 the *kulaks* were deprived of the franchise, excluded from participation in the collectives, and as a class were "liquidated." By 1930 the writer found them eliminated from every district he visited. Those who obstructed collectivization were imprisoned, shot, or exiled to the virgin soil of Siberia or the North, others were dispossessed and left as laborers, or to till small holdings often under tremendous handicaps. Frequently no mercy was shown to a class regarded as their enemies, even though some of them had been merely industrious and thrifty and therefore prosperous. A decree of January 6, 1930, quickened "the pace of collectivization." Local authorities, aided by "shock brigades" of industrial workers from the cities, were sent to collectivize the farms. In fear or opposition many peasants killed their cattle before entering the collectives, at great loss to the country.[1] Under economic and at times

---

[1] Yakovlev, Commissary for Agriculture, admits that last year owing to this catastrophe horned cattle decreased by one-fifth, sheep by one-third, and pigs by two-fifths. Report at Party Congress, 1930.

even military pressure the land was so rapidly and almost forcibly collectivized that by March, 1930, it was estimated that 55 per cent of all peasant farms had been thus organized.[1] The movement, often crude and premature, produced some unfavorable reaction and decrease in membership. By March 2, 1930, Stalin warned his followers that they were suffering with "dizziness from success," and that the movement against the "middle peasants" must be voluntary and not repressive.[2]

Under the new plan there are at present three prevailing types of agriculture—state farms, collectives and individual holdings. The object of the state farms is to furnish an example of model farming to the rest, and to produce grain for government export. By October 1, 1930, there were 3,252 state farms, with an area of over 15,000,000 acres, containing a little over 3 per cent of the acreage of arable land. These were already using over 10,000 tractors and 1550 combines. Six million families, or about one-quarter of the whole peasant population, were united in collectives, while some twenty million families were still cultivating individual farms. In the spring sowing 37.5 per cent of the crops were in collective farms. In the Volga region, taking the average yield of the individual farmer as 100, the per capita yield in the collectives was 133.8, in the communes 153.2, on the government farms 147.7. The whole weight of the government is thrown into making collective farming

---

[1] *Izvestia,* March 14, 1930.

[2] *Izvestia,* April 3, 1930, *Russia's Agrarian Problem,* p. 198, quoted by Foreign Policy Association.

a success. By economy of power and of labor, by expert management, the supply of credit, machinery, seed selection, the lightening of taxes, social service and insurance—by all means cooperation and socialization are encouraged, while individual profiteering is discouraged, taxed, disfranchised or placed without the law.

At the end of the second year of the five year plan on October 1, 1930, the grain crop amounted to 86,500,000 tons, or an increase of 20.6 per cent over the previous year, while the grain for market was 32.6 per cent above the estimate called for by the plan. The collective farms planted 90,000,000 acres in the second year instead of the 51,000,-000 acres called for in the fifth or closing year of the plan. In the principal grain belt 43.8 per cent of the peasants had already joined the collectives while some 12,000,000 acres were already under cultivation in the state grain farms. Consequently this combined "socialized sector" is already producing over 50 per cent of the marketable grain, against only 43 per cent called for in the fifth year of the plan.

The whole of Russia may almost be regarded as one vast experimental farm. In general, collectives are of three prevailing types—the partnership, the artel and the commune. The simplest is the partnership where the peasants unite in the joint cultivation of their land, the use of machinery and horses, although these remain the individual property of the members. In the more usual and successful type of artel the members pool their land, machinery and draft-animals, but retain personal possession of their homes and small livestock. In the commune, or more advanced type, which is not at present so popular with the majority but may become the prevailing plan of the future, the members unite all their resources, and establish communal kitchens, dining rooms, nurseries, laundries, etc.

The individualistic peasant unfamiliar with the new methods, suspicious of change and fearing to lose his private possessions and liberty, may hold aloof for a time. He may naturally fear a new serfdom if he sacrifices his individual holding and is merged in the new collective. He is safeguarded, however, at two points. As a laborer on the state farms he becomes a member of a powerful trade union which is integral to the whole organization of the state. As a member of the self-governing collective he has a vote and voice in the regular open meetings of the community, and a vote in the election or recall of the officers and committee in charge of the organization. So far as the working class is concerned the system is basically democratic. Even Stalin is dependent at every point upon their continued approval. There is of course no democracy and often little justice for those who do not belong to the working class. Credit is socialized for the approved workers. The 9000 local branches of the Central Agricultural Bank throughout rural Russia are ready to advance needed capital on favorable terms payable in from three to five years. This is chiefly available for collectives and those who work in harmony with the government plans. Life is often made unbearably hard for those who do not.

During the summers of 1929 and 1930, the writer visited the villages and endeavored to make a study of this important agricultural movement in the model state farms, the more newly organized collectives where the peasants share only their land and labor, and the more advanced communes where they have all their possessions in common.

In the first commune visited in the Tambov region we stood upon the old ruined watch tower from which the former landlord of the great estate had had his serfs closely watched at their work with a spy glass. Nearby was a building erected by unpaid, forced labor and the whipping post where the former serfs or peasants were chastised when necessary. Here in the commune today are men who once worked for the old Russian general who had owned the estate and bred race horses in its great stables. In Czarist times these peasants in their bitter poverty were paid ten and twelve cents a day, three dollars a month or some forty dollars a year. The watch tower now lies in ruins; the serfs were liberated in 1861; the peasants were liberated from the iniquitous Czarist régime only in 1917.

Today this estate is a commune founded by fifty Russian immigrants who returned from the United States to their own country in 1921. They started with nothing but their bare hands and these empty buildings. The first year they were so poor that they were reduced to eating crows and at times even weeds. Eight years ago their total assets, apart from the land, were $10,000; today they are $60,000. The membership has grown from 50 to 238 persons operating fourteen hundred acres.

Their nine modern tractors are working night and day on three eight-hour shifts. We noticed that one of them was operated by a woman. They have a large herd of cattle as well as several hundred sheep and hogs. They are unusually successful in breeding horses. They have good orchards, a flour and lumber mill, and they are putting in an electric plant. The radio in the social room connects them with Moscow. The members of the commune receive an initial cash payment of fifty or sixty cents a day. Out of this they pay seventeen cents for their board and set a very good table. Their children are cared for, from birth if desired, in the nursery for infants up to the age of four, afterward in kindergarten and school, and finally, for those who are capable, right through the university, from which four have already graduated. They seem particularly successful in their care of the children. We had never seen any who were happier or better trained to cooperate.

The commune is as busy as a beehive and is rapidly extending its work through social service in the surrounding country. It has organized and is organically related to twelve collectives in the region. These embrace some 1800 members, already cultivating over 7000 acres. In the commune they share everything in the cooperative life. In the collective, which may later develop into a commune if successful, they share only land and labor. This commune of 238 members was taxed last year only ninety-two dollars, which is less than the tax of a single rich peasant, probably less than farmers pay in any other country in the world.

Nearby we found individual peasants cultivating their small strips of ten or twelve acres by archaic methods. Their wooden plow was not far in advance of that used by Abraham four thousand years ago, save that it had an iron point, or a broken spade, in place of the primitive sharpened stick. We found them still reaping with a sickle and threshing their grain by hand with a wooden flail, living in mud huts, with straw roofs and mud floors, which they share with the few domestic animals the more fortunate possess. The whole policy of the Government is to discourage individual accumulation of private property and to develop social accumulation in cooperative agriculture. The process of socialization is going on at terrific speed. We visited their new village schools where the children were singing the stirring songs of the Revolution. We saw their busy soviet headquarters and the crowded cooperative stores selling articles at only two per cent profit. The few private stores that are left sell at more than double the price of the cooperatives. We heard individual peasants bitterly complaining of hard times, heavy taxes, and seizures of grain, but always admitting that at the worst they are better off than under the unforgotten oppressions of Czarism. We heard the members of the collectives talking of their privileges, lightened taxes, modern machinery, larger crops and increase of personal comforts and a higher standard of living.

We next visited the Lenin Commune near by. A generation ago the more enterprising of the impoverished workers who could escape left Czarist Russia in despair. All the best land in the region was held by a few rich landlords, while the worst was worked by the peasants. Here was Stephen who had just met us at the train. At the age of eighteen he left the farm where he was earning but five cents a day, journeying on foot, crept across the German border at night to escape from the Czarist régime and emigrated to America. There he earned as high as twelve dollars a day in war time. He joined the Communist Party in America under the leadership of John Reed of Harvard University and was arrested and put in jail as a radical. In spite of high wages he did not feel free under what seemed to him a system of social injustice in the United States. After the Revolution he had dreams of a new day in Russia. In 1922 fifty-two of these Russian workers pooled their savings and with a combined capital of $30,000 purchased agricultural machinery and supplies and returned to Russia to found a colony, just as the fifty whom we had met in the neighboring commune had done the year before.

They were given over 2000 acres of land by the Soviet Government and they founded the Lenin Commune which now, seven years later, numbers some four hundred and fifty persons. The value of their plant and invested capital, apart from the land, has increased during this period from $20,000 to over $170,000. Their net profit last year was about $8,000 after paying all expenses and taxes. They borrow money from the cooperative banks at six and nine per cent interest. After paying all common expenses a small cash bonus accrues to each member. They do not object to the possession of personal property, but all functional property, which is the means of production, is held in common.

Each member of this commune receives from forty to fifty cents a day in wages, from which he pays twenty cents for board. The commune supports all the children of the community, from birth, save for the period of nursing, if desired, providing a pre-school nursery up to the age of four, a kindergarten from the age of four to seven, a school from seven years and upward, and sees the most capable children through college or university, where ten of them are now studying.

Parents and children are in their homes only at night. The home is preserved but some of its functions are performed by the school and others by the community. The center of gravity has shifted from the individual and the separate home to the community. In play and work cooperation becomes a life habit. It is a new way of life. From birth to death their whole training is not to get on in a struggle for individual acquisition and possession, but for the welfare of the whole community. Social acquisition takes the place of individual hoarding. We were impressed by the fact that of all the men with whom we talked who had been in America and had tasted what was to them the flesh pots of prosperity and high wages, not one wanted to go back. There was not a man, and very few of the women and children, but preferred what *they* considered the spiritual values of a greater freedom, self-expression and self-realization in this cooperative community to the greater personal gain and individual possession that they could have in America. They felt that America had taught them much, but that socially they could achieve more in Russia. None seemed to take advantage of the commune as an excuse for laziness. They had found only one slacker in seven years and he was quickly eliminated. The injunction of scripture, "if a man will not work neither shall he eat," was adopted in their constitution.

This commune has its own orchards, dairy, cheese factory, flour mill, foundry, sawmill and common dining room where they share an excellent table. Their cultural life centers in a large club house with its electrical installation, its radio, weekly motion picture, theatricals, and recreational and educational features. During the winter months the whole community engages in study in the evening, as in the people's schools of Denmark. The reading room furnishes a hundred and thirty-five papers and periodicals. In this commune only 27 members belong to the Communist Party and the local government is administered by a soviet or local committee of five, elected annually. Among the youth 32 belong to the Komsomols and 45 to the younger Pioneers, or members of the organized youth movement, busily engaged in active service and preparation for the much coveted membership in the Communist Party. There are practically no special privileges for party members, but greatly increased responsibilities for service.

During the three nights we were present most interesting meetings were held in the club house. The first was a war meeting for the registration of volunteers in case of war with China over the North Manchurian Railway controversy. Throughout Russia the population was exercised over press reports of a series of alleged insults, seizures by the Chinese of Soviet offices and officials, of telegraph and railway lines, and they were convinced that the great powers were behind this series of hostile acts. The highest Chinese officials could not defend these seizures as legal when the writer talked with them later in the year.

Here in the Lenin Commune when volunteers were asked for in case of a possible war with China, in addition to the fourteen who were of draft age, twenty young men and women offered themselves for service. No candidates are ever called for any service or office unless they are open for both sexes equally. It would almost start another revolution if any monopoly of privilege were proposed "for men only." On the first night one man alone in all the commune said he would not go to war. He had also failed to subscribe a month's wages for the third industrial loan that was to make possible the national five year program. Accordingly a meeting of the commune was held on the second night when we were present and he was tried and excluded from membership.[1] After giving him a fair hearing the action was almost unanimous.

On the third evening in the commune a youth meeting was held which was attended by the entire community. Earnest addresses were delivered and the meeting was followed by the weekly motion picture. Most of these are Russian films furnished by the Government. They are not produced for profit but for the education of the people in the ideas they wish to inculcate. The film we saw was on the Springtime of Youth. Visualized in story form it carried a message on education, character and service. The

---

[1] A year later, in 1930, we found that this man had been readmitted to the commune.

climax of the picture never depicts personal achievement, wealth or individual happiness, but some social victory for the community. No films of doubtful influence are allowed in Russia. Douglas Fairbanks is popular but most American films are not up to Russian social standards. Of all theatres charging admission, 40 per cent are operated by trade unions, 35 per cent by the Department of Education, 3 per cent by a Government corporation and only 1 per cent by private persons. This is the one country that has not commercialized the moving picture but made it a vast educational project.

Sunday in the commune was a day of rest. We found but two old women, over seventy, who still occasionally attended church in the neighboring village. In place of the old religion of formalism and esthetic mysticism, often divorced from intelligence, morality and practical life, communists have instead sought to create a new humanitarian religion of social service. Their new moral code at present is a rational system of personal liberty based on social welfare. All marriages in the village are registered. There are few divorces and little irregularity or dissipation in this wholesome socialized village life. Drinking, which was very common among the members of the commune when they lived in America, is now largely eliminated. A nationwide campaign of education is being carried on against drink. The youth seemed healthy, wholesome and self-controlled. The boys and girls of the commune who live in the neighboring city while attending high school are under the guidance of no matron or older person, but maintain a wholesome self-discipline under their own self-governing youth organizations which have a liberal but serious moral code.

Upon returning to Russia in 1930 we found that the two communes mentioned above had been united. Their membership had increased to over a thousand. New features had been introduced. Of several incubators they were operating, one alone was capable of hatching thirty thousand chickens at a time. The exact production of the nationally needed grain, vegetables, dairy products, cattle, sheep, hogs, poultry and every agricultural or industrial product is provided for in the "planned economy" of the State Planning Commission and of the Supreme Economic Council. Nothing is left to chance or to the private profit of anarchic competitive individualism.

Of the members of the commune who formerly lived in America we found that the large majority preferred their present mode of living. They feel that the principal gain in collective and socialized agriculture is in the greater security of life. In America they found high wages were interspersed with unemployment and times of need. There each Russian felt himself an alien. Here he is sure of work, he is never thrown out into helpless unemployment, and can live a full life not dependent on an individual employer. He has his vote and voice in determining all the conditions of his life. New thoughts and aspirations are released within him by the Revolution. If he is an idealist he feels that here he is a part of a great plan and that he is working, not only for himself, but for the benefit of the whole. For him Russia socially seemed the promised land of the future, and not America with its opportunity for private wealth.

The Giant farm in the Caucasus began with half a million acres of virgin steppe land or prairie that had been used for grazing and was now to become a "grain factory." In the first year, 1929, it produced 50,000 tons of wheat from a third of its area. For hours you may drive in an automobile through one vast sea of waving grain that stretches away to the horizon, without houses or trees to break the landscape. In the center are a few administrative buildings for the giant tractors, combines and other machinery. During the very first year 50,000 peasants visited the Giant farm which furnishes a model and proves an inspiration to them to join the collectives. More and more they are uniting in ever larger and more efficient units for mass production.

Even more effective is "Soviet Farm, No. 2," near Rostov on the Don in the Northern Caucasus. This farm covers some 275,000 acres of land which was an uncultivated steppe or prairie less than two years ago. Today it is not only a vast and successful farm, but it also has a college for training engineers for the new mechanized agriculture of the collective farms, with a teaching staff of 70 and 525 students in its "Institute of Engineer Mechanics of Socialist Agriculture."

These state farms had originally to furnish the government an amount of grain equal to what the *kulaks* or rich peasants had produced, approximately 1,800,000 tons. By next year these farms will yield twice that amount. They are now to grapple with the enormous task of repairing the deficiency of the country in meat, milk, butter, vegetables, cotton and flax by state enterprises similar to the successful Grain Trust. As collective cattle breeding will take years to develop, they are also speeding up the rapid raising of pigs by American methods. Thousands of silo towers and tens of thousands of silo trenches are being built in a whirlwind campaign to supply fodder. This year $85,000,000 are being invested in pig sties, and pigs and cattle for breeding. A state trust for cattle is to have three million head in 1931 and thirty-seven million acres of pasture land. Another is to have five million sheep, while 250 farms are being started for pigs. State farms expanded nearly fourfold last year and now cover a total of 12,000,000 acres. The total amount of land under cultivation was increased by some 20,000,000 acres.

An expert of the London *Economist,* after a thorough study of the whole agricultural situation, reports that Russian production of agricultural machinery in 1930 was approximately $160,000,000, or five times the pre-war amount, and that it will likely soon surpass even the United States.[1] The annual output of tractor power in Russia will amount to three million horsepower from the factories now under construction, and will be ready for the mechanical cultivation of over 200,000,000 acres. The expert of the *Economist* was deeply impressed with the "efficiency, strict discipline, natural friendliness and camaraderie" and the youth of the staff in the great farms mentioned above, who

---

[1] See *The Economist,* Russian Supplement, November 1, 1930, to which we are indebted in this section.

were practically all under thirty. He found them in a revolutionary epoch where everything seems possible. They now contemplate moving the whole wheat belt up to the confines of Asia, where roughly a thousand million acres can be cultivated by American methods, and then utilize the present wheat region for more valuable and intense cultivation. The young Commissary of Agriculture reports that by the spring of 1933 they will have an additional sixty million acres under cultivation in the semi-drought zone where one man with his machines will look after 500 acres.[1]

The English expert found that the peasants were accepting the profitable program of industrialization and mechanization, but there may yet be a battle against the encroachments of the collectives upon their social, religious and family life. This is likely to create a rift between the older and younger generations. Parents still want to receive payment of their daughters' wages and retain their old customs. But the cultural upheaval of the collective movement has brought new liberty and privileges to youth. Farm boys can now produce electric light and pumps for irrigation for local market gardens. They enter schools for tractor and motor driving and find a rich social life without migrating to the city. They enter the courses for the "liquidation of illiteracy," organize fire brigades, enjoy the new social centers, the radio and cinema moving platforms.

---

[1] It is proposed to divide the whole country into five zones as follows: 1. Technical crops, cotton, tobacco, hemp, sugar beets, corn, soya beans, etc.; 2. flax, dairy produce, market gardening; 3. sub-tropical cotton, tea, grapes, oranges, fruits; 4. extensive stock breeding; 5. forests occupying one-quarter of the country. *The Economist*, Nov. 1, 1930.

Youth accepts enthusiastically the new mode of life and is finding a place for leadership in the agricultural revolution.

Youth, age and the government all must adapt themselves and yield something to the new movement. The government has not been able to maintain the idea of complete equality in the collectives. They permit a five per cent dividend on capital invested. Some have their own cows, pigs, poultry and vegetable gardens. The distribution of profits depends upon quantity and quality of labor contributed. Upon the basis of a five-grade tariff, the best paid jobs go to the most skilled men. The system is not, however, producing petty, private capitalists, but rather social wealth and shared privilege. The ablest lead and receive something for their special work, but there is still a democratic, substantial equality maintained. All risks are shared and the individual, sustained by the community, is not driven in fear to lay up for himself against the hazards of the future. The system is developing both individual initiative and social security.

A new peasantry is being evolved in Russia. The revolution has given the peasant the land and a new liberty. It has in many ways driven him from the old ruts. It has swept over him with a cyclone of new ideas and practices. Whether he accepts them or resists them, his children at least have broken from the old order. They bring home daily new suggestions from the school or youth meeting. There are new posters, new motion pictures, new institutions, new agricultural methods all about him. He sees the tractors plowing their deep furrows about his little

farm. He sees the larger crops and better living standard
of his neighbors who have joined the collectives. He and
his friends attend the village meeting. They are elected
on the soviets and other committees. They learn to speak
out and fight for their rights as they never dared to do
under Czarist oppression. However painful the process of
transition for those of the older generation who cannot or
will not change their habits of life, a new day has dawned
for Russia. Probably greater changes are taking place
among the peasants in this single decade than in the last
two thousand years upon these steppes.

One of the great experiments of the world is being tried
out in Russia today—the experiment of a united, cooperative, socialized order, in contrast to competitive, individualistic, nationalistic states. Dogmatists on both sides may
scout with contempt the possibility of an experiment in any
but their own orthodox way of life. History may decide
between the two. Or, it may evolve elements of value in
each that can exist side by side; or it may enable both to
make a lasting contribution in a higher synthesis of experience.

The American agricultural expert, Mr. A. A. Johnson,
estimates that if the present rate of progress is maintained,
within ten years Russia will be the greatest producer and
exporter of grain in the world. As one travels over the
great plains of central Russia or the steppes of the South,
he sees endless reaches of some of the most fertile soil in
the world. Nevertheless, after centuries the inhabitants
had been left impoverished, unable to conquer the land with

their bare hands. Today that untamed desert of potential wealth is being made to blossom as the rose. As far as the eye can reach, in the great state farms and collectives, there seems to appear an unbroken oasis, a golden stretch of ripened grain. This vast and rapidly extending plan of industrialized agriculture is changing not only the economic conditions of an age-long poverty; it is transforming the physical landscape and, even more important, the mental psychology of the peasant as well.

Thus, in the course of one or two decades Russian agriculture is becoming rapidly industrialized and socialized, cooperative and collective. It is indeed one of the most significant experiments in the world.

CHAPTER IV

INDUSTRY AND LABOR

One of Russia's most conspicuous successes lies in the field of industry. By 1921 industrial production had fallen to 17 per cent of that of pre-war figures, and agricultural production to 52 per cent.[1] Stalin was able to report to the Sixteenth Party Congress in June, 1930, that in less than a decade industrial production had been raised from 17 to 180 per cent of the pre-war maximum.[2] Within a decade, by 1931, it will have exceeded 200 per cent. An advance of more than tenfold in production in a decade, in the face of a world depression and without foreign loans, is unprecedented. With production, the basic wealth invested in industry had also annually grown during the decade, usually from 12 to 25 per cent a year. The Soviets had taken over an agricultural country, where 82 per cent of the population were backward peasants, and where there were less factories in all Russia than in the single state of Pennsylvania. Even today there are only

---

[1] Professor Gromann of the Gosplan at the Geneva Industrial Conference, *Soviet Russia in the Second Decade,* p. 41. By 1921 the output of mineral fuels and metal ores had stopped almost completely. The number of workers had decreased to 60 per cent of pre-war, and real wages amounted hardly to 35 per cent. *Gosplan, The Soviet Union Looks Ahead,* p. 8.

[2] *Pravda,* June 29, 1930.

some 5,221,000 industrial factory workers out of a total population of 160,000,000, or about 3 per cent in Russia compared to over 8 per cent in the United States. The problem was to industrialize and socialize this backward agricultural country.[1]

Russia presents today the novel picture of a socialized state, where the profit motive as it is known in America has almost ceased to operate. No private person can legitimately make a profit out of the system of state and co-operative economy. The ownership of all land and natural resources, more than 90 per cent of industrial production, all foreign trade, railways, large banks, and more than nine-tenths of the total trade turnover is already socialized. This is the most colossal experiment in socialism ever attempted.

All of industry is organized and operated in several hundred so-called state trusts. A trust usually manages a group of mines or factories in a given region. They are state organizations operating under the Supreme Economic Council, for the efficient management of industry upon a self-supporting basis, if possible earning profit for the

---

[1] In 1909 the per capita production for all industrial products was but $160, compared to $2,280 in the United States; up to the time of the war the per capita value of agricultural products in Russia was but $30, compared to $200 in the United States. The theoretical aim and the titanic practical problem was to unify the whole of Russia's economic life under a single scientific plan, to socialize all basic resources and production, to eliminate private profit and therefore all conflicting class interests, to organize the whole working population in socially useful labor, to provide for the active participation of the workers in the whole economic and political life.

state. The strong and profitable trusts are thus made to support the backward or undeveloped industries.[1]

Russia is the only country which has the distinction of bringing its whole economy—industry, agriculture, and trade; production, consumption and distribution, under the perview of a single economic general staff. It is called the Gosplan, or State Planning Commission. This is neither an executive nor an administrative body, but furnishes the general strategy and plan for Russia's whole economic life. It somewhat resembles the Allied General Staff, or President Wilson's War Industries Board. There are some 500 experts on the central staff, headed by a governing board of sixteen.

Its first aim was to bring Russia's economic output up to the pre-war basis and make the country self-supporting. Next it seeks, by a series of annual and five-year plans, to accomplish economically the seemingly impossible, by the enthusiastic cooperation of all producers, consumers and officials, after the elimination of all conflict between employers and employed, where the classes of owners and dependents have now ceased to exist. All are workers in a workers' state. The Gosplan aims at a goal of the maxi-

---

[1] The trust may be vertical, including one given industrial process, like woodworking, or horizontal, like the Sugar Trust, which includes everything from the growing of beets to the marketing of sugar. Each trust is legally independent, responsible for its own financial obligations. It is subject to universal labor laws and settles its wage rates through collective bargaining with the trade unions. Of the profits, about 50 per cent go to the government, 10 to 14 per cent for the welfare of the workers, while the balance is devoted to the surplus of the trust for expansion and reserves.

mum production of necessities and plain comforts, by a minimum of human effort, while seeking first the human factor of the health, safety, education, cultural development and optimum working conditions for all who labor. Of the 75,394,000 gainfully employed, 60,676,000 are in agriculture and only 5,221,000 in industry proper, including large and small scale, although there are now 10,887,000 urban workers.[1]

The Five-Year Plan

The whole life of Russia at present is centered in the five year plan which is the most titanic undertaking of the Soviet Union. The plan aims to transform Russia from a prevailingly agricultural into a genuinely industrial nation with a self-sufficient and balanced economy. Between October 1, 1928, and September 30, 1933, this seemingly impossible transformation is to take place. The whole constitutes nothing less than a deliberate and directed industrial revolution.

---

[1] In agriculture 60,696,000
Large scale industry 2,864,000
Small scale industry 2,357,000
Construction 725,000
Transportation 560,000
Telegraph and telephone 93,000
Trade 1,163,000
Education 753,000
Health service 366,000
State and Cooperatives 922,000
Miscellaneous 3,895,000

75,394,000

Michael B. Scheler in *Current History,* October, 1930, p. 47.

Thus far the yearly goal of the plan has not only been equalled but exceeded in most branches of industry, so that some of the goals set for 1933 had been surpassed by October, 1930. In two fields the plan fell short at the beginning, and will probably be uneven in its accomplishments. At the close of the first year the decrease in cost of production was only 5 per cent instead of the scheduled 7 per cent; while labor productivity was increased 14.5 per cent instead of the 17.3 per cent called for by the plan.[1] An increase of wages by 10.5 per cent and the reduction of the average working day to 7.2 hours made these goals more difficult.

At the close of the five-year period the gross agricultural output is expected to be 155 per cent of that of 1927-28, that of all industries is to be 236 per cent, power capacity 324 per cent, and power output 451 per cent of 1927-28, or eleven times the pre-war standard.[2] And all this is attempted by Russia alone, without foreign loans or aid, in the midst of world depression, after having lifted herself out of seemingly hopeless chaos and bankruptcy.

During the first year, 1928-29, more than a hundred new industrial establishments were completed. Colonel Hugh Cooper, the American hydroelectric power plant construction engineer, builder of the Muscle Shoals project, is now chief consultant for the building of the even larger $100,-000,000 combination dam and electrical station on the River

---

[1] *Current History*, July, 1930, p. 653.

[2] *Ibid*, p. 652. The year 1927-28 means from October 1, 1927 to October 1, 1928.

Dnieper. Of some ten thousand engineers, technicians and skilled workers from foreign lands now working in Russia, nearly a thousand are from America, with a larger number from Germany. The important Turkestan-Siberian Railway, over 1100 miles in length, connecting the southern cotton belt with the granary of Siberia, was completed in April, 1930, over a year ahead of schedule. Its builder, Shatoff, was a member of the I. W. W. in the United States for whom America could offer no better place than a jail. In Russia he was recognized at once as an able banker and railway builder. Three large automobile factories are under construction, one of which, under the technical assistance of the Ford Motor Company, is to produce 140,-000 cars yearly, while a fourth factory plans to produce 160,000 cars. Two large tractor plants, with a production of 50,000 units each, are now being built.

Aviation is to share in the five-year plan with an investment of $50,000,000. Already Russia has twenty air lines, covering 16,000 miles and annually carrying 11,476 passengers. At the close of the five-year period they expect to have 145 lines, covering 80,000 miles, and carrying 300,000 passengers annually. This would slightly exceed the present passenger traffic in American aviation. The writer's experience of flying in Russia convinced him of the growing efficiency of the system of aviation.

The enormous increase in electrification and in the metal and machine industries are basic to the whole plan. At one of their weakest points and with the greatest difficulty the plan contemplates increasing the output of pig iron, which in the pre-war period was four million tons, to ten million tons by 1933. The pre-war output of coal has already been doubled.[1] Oil, electrification and agricultural engineering have more than fulfilled the requirements of the original plan and of the revised figures.[2] The Russians remember Lenin's formula that "electrification plus soviets equals socialism." Electric power is their pet hobby, yet the rapid development of industry and the need for power ever outstrips the growing output. The production of agricultural machinery increased 54 per cent last year and is already five times the pre-war output.

A new chemical industry is being created. An era of titanic building is in evidence all over Russia—factories, dams, hydroelectric power stations, irrigation plants, railways, oil wells, mining projects, vast agricultural centers for state farms and collectives, and housing for industrial workers. About 35 per cent of the total industrial output will come from the newly constructed plants. Nearly three billion dollars is to be invested in urban housing. This is desperately needed. Moscow is the most overcrowded city in the world. But model houses are now being built in all cities and in many new farming centers.

The five-year plan provided for total new investments of

---

[1] Pre-war 23 million tons, 1929–30 46 million tons. *The Economist,* November 1, 1930. Statistics in this section were originally taken from *The Five Year Plan for Economic Construction* or *The Soviet Union Looks Ahead,* 1929. Many of its estimates had already been surpassed by October 1, 1930. Electric power production is to reach 22 billion kilowatt-hours a year, coal production 75 million tons, oil 23 million tons, pig iron 10 million tons, chemical fertilizers 7 million tons by 1933.

[2] The production of oil increased in the first two years 14.4 and 26 per cent and was 14,000,000 tons in the latter year.

$33,300,000,000, including some $8,500,000,000 for industry, $12,000,000,000 for agriculture and the remainder for transportation, electrification and housing. Even this is being increased so that at the close of the five-year period there will probably have been an expenditure of some $50,-000,000,000. This means the staggering undertaking of setting aside half the national income for five years. Probably no other society could attempt it. The accumulation and redistribution of wealth on such a scale is unprecedented in economic history.

Unemployment was reduced from 1,714,000 in 1929 and 1,080,000 early in 1930 until there was no registered unemployment at the end of 1930 but a real scarcity of labor in building, industry and agriculture. The productivity of labor is expected to increase 110 per cent in industry while there is to be an estimated increase in money wages of 47 per cent in five years, and in real wages an increase of 70.5 per cent, which will be 108.9 per cent above 1913. The average working day will be 6.86 hours, or 3.03 hours shorter than in 1913.

It is planned that the goods famine is to be ended within the five-year period. The national income is to be increased from 12.3 billion dollars to 24.8 billion dollars computed at constant prices, or 103 per cent. This means an annual increase of over 10 per cent, compared to the greatest known increase in the United States between 1880 and 1890 of 4.5 per cent a year.[1]

---

[1] Tugan-Baranovsky, *The Russian Factory,* and G. M. Price, *Labor Protection in Soviet Russia,* pp. 15–20.

The five-year plan is steadily socializing trade. In 1923, after two years of the New Economic Policy, 90 per cent of retail trade was in the hands of private dealers. Then the unthinking world said that Russia had been forced to abandon communism as a failure and was turning back to capitalism. When the government became strong enough "Nepmen" were taxed out of existence. In the first year of the plan trade was divided as follows: private 13.9 per cent, cooperatives 48.5, the State 37.6. In the fifth year of the plan, 1932-33, they have reason to expect the following proportions: private 3.2, cooperatives 59.2, the State 37.6.

Motivation for sustained enthusiasm in connection with the plan becomes a problem for the leaders, but they seem to be solving it. The feverish "tempo" they believe is possible for them under socialism where it would be impossible under capitalism. The trait of enthusiasm for quantity rather than quality, for expansion rather than intensification is called in Russia "Americanism." Nothing is counted impossible. Work is speeded up by a socialist "emulation" campaign where groups of workers in one factory enter into competition with those in another to increase production. These competitions take on the enthusiastic character of an American football season. In addition to public approval and praise there are substantial rewards and prizes, always, however, social rather than personal. The AMO factory in Moscow, which exceeded its quota, received a prize of $375,000 for the purpose of building model houses for the workers. The Laps factory was awarded $250,000 for the same purpose. The Marx factory in Leningrad received $375,000; the Lenin Mine secured $150,000 for housing. At the Ilytch Metallurgical Works six workers received travelling scholarships abroad.

Wartime methods "to win the war" are utilized in a dramatic and intense motivation, with a sense of practically equal sharing in a vast social undertaking, a feeling of real ownership in social wealth and a wide distribution of responsibility. For all who will lead or work the country is theirs. It is under the influence of such a spirit that the government dares to undertake in five years the hitherto unheard-of herculean task of doubling the national income and trebling industrial production. Even if these figures are heavily discounted they compare more than favorably with the United States where the rate of increase in productivity has been about 4 per cent a year in normal times. Experts like those of *The Economist* of London, the leading financial weekly in the principal capitalist center of the world, bear testimony to the amazing success of the plan as a whole despite its many shortcomings.

There are many faults and failures in the plan, however. As a titanic, sacrificial undertaking it places a strain upon the entire nation. It is a bed of roses for none. The plan is often made an end in itself. Quality is frequently sacrificed to quantity and is often pitifully poor. Machinery, hastily installed, sometimes will not function. Production is uneven and backward portions of the plan delay others.

The leaders are enthusiastic but the workers sometimes suffer from "war weariness." The very success of the plan entails real privation. Under capitalism an economic crisis is usually due to over-production while Russia chronically suffers from under-production. The government has no selling problem. Instead, the whole population might almost be pictured as standing in line waiting to be served. The shortage is connected with the enormous rapidly growing internal market, ever developing new wants, the organization of the consumers, and the control by the government of both producers and consumers and their finances.[1]

The "tempo" declined somewhat in the second year of the plan. After the first year increase in production was 23.4 per cent, or 2 per cent above the goal. The second year did not realize the further anticipated increase of 31 per cent but was maintained at 24 per cent above the preceding year, compared to a 4 per cent advance in annual industrial production in the United States. The closing quarter of 1930 was a critical "shock period" during which Moscow expected "every man to do his duty."

The "fluidity" of labor constitutes another problem where thousands move from one job and one region to another in search of better food conditions or higher pay. American engineers and technicians working in Russia have often met with physical hardships in their living conditions. But even more annoying has been the slipshod methods and poor labor discipline of many of the Russian workers, and the lack of responsibility and authority of managers and

---

[1] See *The Economist,* London, November 1, 1930, to which we are indebted here. The demand may however be free from the fluctuation of a capitalist market. The buyers are conveniently reduced to half a dozen such as the Grain Trust, the Tractor Center, the Cotton Grower, the Kolhos or Collective Center, etc.

foremen in getting things done promptly and efficiently and in operating the new factories which have been so hastily erected. Yet by trial and error, by failure as well as success, the Russians are learning.

In their reports to the Sixteenth Congress of the Communist Party in July, 1930, Stalin and Kuibishev, President of the Supreme Economic Council, dealt with present attainments rather than with future prophecy.[1] Their basic capital has been doubled in three years. What other country could say as much during a period of world depression? The labor productivity of the casual Slav has increased 41 per cent in three years, and was 50 per cent higher than in 1913. While in two years agricultural production had increased to 113 per cent of the pre-war maximum, the annual industrial production in the second year of the plan, 1929-30, was 180 per cent of pre-war production, and transportation 193 per cent. The value of production increased during last year 76 per cent in strategic industries and 24 per cent in agriculture over the preceding year. It was but a short time ago that Secretary Hughes called Russia an "economic vacuum." No country is less of a vacuum today.

At the close of the second year of the plan on October 1, 1930, Kuibishev was able to report a surprising advance along almost the entire economic front, which had more than fulfilled the goals set for this period and now seems to justify the Government in the conviction that they will

---

[1] Stalin's report is in *Pravda*, June 29, 1930; Kuibishev's in *Izvestia*, July 11, 1930.

achieve the five-year plan in four years.[1]   The pre-war level of industrial production already had been doubled.

The gains in the various fields compared to the goals set are as follows:

	Output 1929–30	Estimate of Plan	Percentage of Excess over Plan
Oil	30,600,000 tons	28,000,000 tons	9.6
Steel	10,200,000 tons	9,900,000 tons	3.
Rolled Metal	8,300,000 tons	7,600,000 tons	9.2
Electro-technical output	$390,500,000	$294,000,000	32.6
Agricultural machinery	257,500,000	236,000,000	8.8
Gross Output	25%	20%	5.
Means of production industries	40%	24%	16.

The Trade Unions

The trade unions in Russia are naturally the largest and strongest of any country in the world.   In the eighteenth century work was based on compulsory labor, the workers being either chattels of the nobles or belonging to villages bought and owned by the industrial employers.   By the nineteenth century free labor began to develop.   Hours of work were from twelve to eighteen a day.

Before the war in Czarist Russia while a kind of "company union" controlled by the police was permitted, all genuine organizations of the workers were suppressed and strikes were broken up with bloodshed.   By the time of the first Revolution there were not more than 1500 union mem-

---

[1] *New York Times,* December 1, 1930.

bers. Today there are nearly 12,000,000, including 95 per cent of all productive workers who are eligible. They are organized in 23 large industrial unions, uniting all the employees in a given industry regardless of their craft or function. The trade unions constitute a basic and integral part of the economic, political and cultural life of the country. Collective bargaining is provided for by the Constitution and all employers of labor, whether state or private, are required to recognize the unions and to negotiate with them. On the other hand, workers' control of factories was found to be a complete failure and nowhere is labor allowed to wield the "big stick" by a monopoly of power, or to disregard the welfare of the public as consumers. Their special privileges, however, are numerous, including protection by labor laws, reduction in payment of taxes, social insurance, rents, tickets for theatres and entertainments, preference in entrance for themselves or their children in educational institutions, free vacations at rest houses and free medical treatment. A trade union card is a priceless possession and its many privileges are attested by the almost maximum membership that is allowed. This is true both of the trade unions and the cooperatives.

The trade union begins in the factory with the shop committee elected annually by all the workers. Its duty is to protect the workers, represent them in all relations with the employer, whether private or state trust, administer the social welfare work of the factory nursery, school, library, hospital or other institutions, increase production, and coordinate the various economic interests of the plant. The trade unions bargain collectively with the state agencies for the fixing of wages.

The right to strike against a private employer or state enterprise is legally provided for but is seldom used, and then only when other forms of negotiation have failed.[1] The sympathy of the state is often with the strikers against the state trust. A complete mechanism is provided for the impartial settlement of all disputes. If a dispute cannot be settled by the shop committee it is referred to an arbitration committee, both parties being represented equally with a neutral chairman. In case of a deadlock, the dispute may be passed on to a Board of Arbitration, whose decision is final. There are no exhaustive struggles over "recognition" or hours of work, which are the shortest in the world.

There is a healthy trade union democracy among the workers. Economically free, independent of any individual employer, apprehensive of no arbitrary discharge or neglected unemployment, the laboring class at least is encouraged in the freedom of expression and the right of criticism of industry or the government. Soviet Russia has a merited reputation for merciless self-criticism. All papers and reports of the trade unions and the Party are full of it. This is confirmed by literally thousands of letters from workers and peasants that pour in to the daily press, the factory wall newspapers, etc. However, action that would be regarded

---

[1] The number of strikes in 1924 and following years was 267, 196, 337, 396, and in 1928, 150, involving a total number of strikers of less than 50,000 a year. This would be but a small fraction of those in the United States in the same years. Strikes are looked upon merely as a lack of coordination between a workers' government and workers' unions.

as seditious for the overthrow of the government would not be permitted in Russia any more than in America and would be dealt with more swiftly and ruthlessly.

Wages in Russia are still confessedly low while the cost of living is relatively high. The writer found in 1923 that the average wage for all Russia was only 25 cents a day. In Moscow wages then ran from $10 to $50 a month. In 1930 the average wage for the U. S. S. R. for unskilled labor was $31.90 a month, and for skilled labor $41.95.[1] In Moscow the average is $46.32, a husband and wife each receiving about the same wage. Real wages are already 16 per cent above those of 1913, with additional benefits and social services amounting to 27.3 per cent of the total payroll, in reduced rents and prices, free vacations, medical service, etc.[1] Professor Paul Douglas estimates that American workers earn about three and a third times those of Russia, and that their standard of living is approximately three and a half times as high.[2]

Colonel C. T. Starr of the American engineering firm of Stuart, James and Cooke, advisor of the Soviet Coal Trusts,

---

[1] Statistics furnished by the Gosplan, August, 1930.
[2] *Soviet Russia in the Second Decade*, p. 241. A Moscow worker would earn, say $40 a month and his wife about the same, or a little less. He pays 2 per cent of his wages to the trade union, $6 a month for rent. He pays at the cooperative 2 cents a pound for black bread, 5 cents for brown. For beef he pays 20 cents a pound, ham 50 cents, Swiss cheese 60 cents, fish 62 cents. His suit of clothes costs $25, a pair of shoes $5 to $10, cotton socks 75 cents, a shirt $2.50, cap $3, an overcoat $30. If the workman is poor his rent, which is the average in Moscow, is only $1.25 a month. He has many perquisites in the way of medical attendance, theatre tickets, social insurance, etc. On the whole he is fairly contented, he works hard, and is indifferent to his food and physical hardships.

reports on the condition of workers in the mines of the Don Basin that wages ranged from 60 cents to $2.00 a day for a working day of from 6 to 8 hours. Vacations on full pay ranged from twelve days to one month. Other compensation, insurance, social service, rent, heat, light and food at reduced prices amount to 37 per cent added to the workers' wages. Every man works four days out of five and has seventy rest days a year. Allowing for these benefits, the average net compensation per worker was a little over $600 a year. Food and housing conditions for Russian workers are still often primitive, but no workers care less for their condition or will put up with more hardship. The strain and self-sacrifice imposed upon the workers by the five-year plan would not be tolerated by independent, individualistic, Anglo-Saxon workers, but, along with some grumbling and complaint, is stolidly borne by the Russian workingmen.

Russia has been lavish in employing such experts as Colonel Starr. Ralph Budd, president of the Great Northern Railway, as technical advisor of Russia's transportation system; Thomas Campbell, who operates the largest farm in America, and hundreds of others have been wisely employed. In industry and agriculture Russia is always eager to learn.

Social Services

In protective labor legislation and social insurance Russia probably leads the world, although the amount of insurance paid to some classes is less, for instance, than in Germany. In 1913 the average number of hours in the normal working day was 9.9. The Labor Code of 1918 and 1922 introduced a maximum eight hour day. Today it has been reduced to an average of 7.2 hours. Instead of one day's rest in seven, one in five is now provided in "the continuous working week." Each worker rests each fifth day, or six days each month. As the workers take their rest in rotation industry never stops. This innovation is not yet popular, however, as the workers like to have their holiday together with all their friends.

The Russian Labor Code is characterized by its universality. It is applicable to all forms of labor in all trades. Employment is a matter of national concern and it is the business of government Labor Exchanges to find work for every possible man. In August 1930, 1,080,900 were unemployed though there was a strong demand for labor and a shortage of it in many rural districts. About half the unemployed received aid from the state insurance funds varying from $6 to $15 a month, according to their skill, former salary, etc., with reduction of rent and other benefits. The rate was lower, however, than in England or Germany. Child labor, which is still permitted in so many of the states in America, is prohibited in Russia for children under fourteen, while those from fourteen to sixteen may work but four hours a day, and from sixteen to eighteen six hours.

Social insurance legislation is more beneficial to the workers in Russia in many respects than in any other country. Already more than nine-tenths of the wage workers are insured. This social insurance is in the control of the trade unions, the Commissariat of Labor and the workers themselves. While in other countries the workers usually contribute from thirty to forty per cent of the insurance funds, in Soviet Russia the workers are not asked to contribute anything. About fourteen per cent of the wages, but not *from* the wages, is devoted to such social insurance, while in most other countries it ranges from two to four per cent.[1] Most generous and extensive provisions for payments for maternity and child welfare, for medical care, for temporary and permanent disability, unemployment, invalidity and old age, housing, death benefit and burial are made. It is evident that low wages are largely compensated for by increased security, reduced rents and prices for food, recreation, cultural privileges, education for the worker and his children and provision for all contingencies and for old age. There is no place in the system for hoarding because of individual fear, to make provision for the unknown future. The risk is shared and borne by all socially instead of individually. The American worker receives higher wages but has less security against unemployment, old age, sickness, etc. The Russian has lower wages but more security. Several hundred labor exchanges at government expense are responsible for providing work for every possible man.

Working women, who were the beasts of burden in old

---

[1] *Labor Protection in Soviet Russia,* by G. M. Price, p. 99. In old Russia 75 per cent of the population was left without medical aid. Today the whole medical profession has been socialized. Medical practitioners are incorporated in the service of the state during five or six hours a day. Beyond this they are free for private practice. Medical treatment in hospitals and homes alike is free for all trade union members and is increasingly on a preventive rather than a curative basis. A growingly successful campaign is waged against drink, venereal disease and prostitution.

Russia, are specially protected and as a rule prohibited from night work and from certain arduous employments. All manual women workers are free from work on full pay eight weeks before and eight weeks after childbirth. Additional financial assistance and special provisions are made for mothers during the seven to nine months nursing period.[1]

Public nurseries, provided for small children whose mothers are at work, are a notable feature of Russian life, not only in the factories, but on the collective farms, and in the parks and places of amusement. Such scientific and uniformly kind treatment of children is all the more noteworthy in a country that was recently so backward.

Among Russia's social institutions is the "red corner" which is a room or corner in a factory or club which provides newspapers, magazines, books, and study courses where cultural work is carried on. In these corners numerous circles and groups meet for study courses in discussions on every conceivable subject. There are station or traveling libraries and motion pictures made available for many of the most distant and isolated places. Excursions at reduced rates for study and recreation and visits to the numerous museums are planned. There are fifty such museums in Moscow alone, some of them of a high educational and cultural value, while others are for propaganda purposes. The

---

[1] Working mothers are maintained in hospital for two weeks after childbirth. After two months' rest on full pay, for nine months following she receives 25 per cent extra on her wages. In all the larger factories here are crèches for the care of the children under expert nurses. See *Soviet Labor Code*, Section 183.

extension of adult education and the fight against illiteracy are notable achievements. No other country in the world has such a comprehensive system of workers' education.

"Wall newspapers" are edited by a group of workers. There are more than a quarter of a million correspondents and writers for the daily press and wall newspapers who make suggestions, ventilate their grievances and by rigorous criticism help to democratize the movement so far as the workers are concerned.

Vacations are provided for workers for at least two weeks on full pay in advance. Palaces and summer resorts of the former nobility are turned over for sanitaria, rest homes, hospitals and nurseries for the workers and their children. In the palace and surrounding park of some former noble-man, one sees accommodated during the course of a single summer several thousand workers in turn. The visitor sees them browning themselves on the lawns in the sun, resting in hammocks under the trees, swimming in the lake or river, or playing games over the wide grounds. It is an almost startling sight to see every former palace, every gallery, resort or place of amusement socialized for the most needy among the workers—children, women, men, the sick, the aged, the infirm. Nearly a million workers are annually taken care of without charge in the mansions and palaces of the former aristocracy, the handful of the privileged class who once possessed the bulk of the wealth, the best land and the special privileges of "holy Russia."

A whole network of clubs, educational and recreational centers is spread throughout Russia. These are never paternalistic, but democratically run by the workers themselves. All principal factories or groups of factories have their clubs where the workers spend their spare hours in reading, study and recreation. There is a room for lectures and entertainments, classrooms for groups, a dining room, billiard and games room, library and reading room, sometimes a gymnasium, an athletic ground and a children's room. Most clubs are equipped with radios and for motion pictures. At the noon hour, in the afternoon and evening these rooms are crowded. In the summer months the workers have their parks, athletic grounds and boat clubs on the rivers and lakes. More than 7000 playgrounds for children are now in operation. In Moscow over ninety such places are open every night in the summer.

As one of these we might visit the single Park of Culture and Rest in Moscow. One may see a hundred thousand workers there every summer afternoon and evening and three hundred thousand on special days. Children of the workers are scientifically cared for free of charge in different departments for every age. We visit the library, reading room and remarkable educational exhibits. Scores are at the chess tables. We attend the free language classes in English and other foreign languages. On the huge athletic field we see a dozen familiar sports in progress. Thirty courts of American volley ball are going side by side. The youth sing out: "There go the Americans. Come and have a game with us." Our group accepts the challenge and we are beaten by a narrow margin, as the good humored crowd applauds with hilarity. The girls then challenge us to a game, confident of victory. In no country are foreigners so little noticed and yet treated with more good will.

On the river we find every trade union has its boat club. There are craft of all types, eight-oared, four-oared and single shells, for boys, girls, and workers of all kinds. Athletics and gymnastics seem to be as popular here as in America or Britain. There is the finest spirit of equal comradeship between the sexes. In no other country have we seen more sensible girls or less petting and spooning.

We observe no round dancing of single couples, but in large open spaces there is folk dancing upon a large scale for young and old. We can hardly keep our feet still as good-natured crowds take their turn, always with music and under trained leadership, in this healthy and hilarious recreation, which seems to have recaptured the spirit of the "merrie England" of the middle ages.

On an evening when all the trade union workers of the country had voluntarily voted a day's pay for speeding up the five year plan, we saw three hundred thousand workers in this park with its free entertainments—opera, theatre, ballet, circus, or moving pictures, all of the highest order, filling and refilling the tents and halls. It was like a vast Coney Island with the addition of educational features and provisions for culture and rest, not commercialized, but run every day and every night in the year by the municipality at a deliberate loss of millions for the benefit of the people. Nowhere in the world have we seen such a park. Yet such playgrounds and institutions, on a smaller and more modest scale, are being standardized and introduced not only in all

the cities but also in some of the most distant country places.
Leisure, rest, recreation and privilege are being socialized as
in no other land.

The Cooperative Movement

The cooperative movement is by far the strongest in the
world.   Indeed it enrolls more members than all the rest of
the world combined.   The early cooperative movement met
with the hostility of the Czar's government which never
gave it legal recognition.   The Soviet Government, on the
other hand, has thrown the whole weight of its power in
favor of the movement and practically controls it.   The
three main forms of cooperation in Russia today are the
Consumers, Agricultural and Handicraft organizations.
The total membership of all Consumers cooperatives on
April 1, 1930, was the enormous total of 42,199,000.   The
Agricultural cooperatives enroll 27,000,000 members, who
also, for the most part, belong to the Consumers organizations.   The Peasant Craft organizations have 1,760,000
members and the Housing cooperatives 762,000.   With the
rapid drift of the rural population to the cities the important
function of these is the collective building and management
of dwellings.   Apart from 6.7 per cent in the cities and the
3.9 per cent of the population in the villages who are disfranchised,[1] nearly all the families of Russia are members
of the cooperatives.

The Consumers societies own and operate 111,238 stores.

---

[1] These include those living on unearned income, members of the Czarist
police, the clergy, and those deprived of civil rights by the courts.

There are local, district, regional and national unions with a central organization, the Centrosoyus, as the administrative center for the whole of the Soviet Union. They have an annual turnover of over eleven billion dollars, which is several times larger than the expenditure of the United States Government or the business of the U. S. Steel Corporation.

The cooperatives conduct some 55 per cent of the wholesale trade of Russia, 62 per cent of the retail trade and 10 per cent of the foreign trade. They buy more than a third of the grain of Russia, 90 per cent of the butter, and sell over 60 per cent of the cotton goods. The Consumers cooperatives supply rural consumers with industrial products, the cities with agricultural produce, and they buy and market the peasants' grain. They deal almost exclusively in necessities. Often the cooperative is the only store in a village, while there are hundreds of them in a single large city. They charge but 2 per cent profit and constitute a gigantic socialized business.

The British and most of the European cooperatives have followed the example of the Rochdale Pioneers in charging market prices and declaring relatively large dividends to the purchasers. The Russian cooperatives, however, sell almost at cost and undersell the private traders from 15 to 30 per cent or more in price. They are given large powers and privileges by the state and in turn offer privileges to their members, where membership is often the only guarantee of getting even a limited supply of articles of which there is a shortage. The future of Russian trade probably belongs increasingly to them. During the last four years their trade turnover has quadrupled, the state trading organizations have doubled, while private trading has grown steadily less, being heavily taxed both at wholesale and retail. In 1923 Lenin said: "The sole remaining task to us has been to secure a real cooperative alliance of the population." The work of the cooperatives is furthered by the Government, the Communist Party and the trade unions. The cooperatives also conduct a wide cultural work.[1]

The Agricultural cooperatives endeavor to fill the same rôle as those of Denmark, though they are not as yet so advanced or effective. They market the peasants' produce, provide machinery and fertilizers, seek to increase production and improve agricultural methods. Their central organization is the Selskosoyus. They sell about one-fifth of the agricultural machinery and market 16.5 per cent of the farmers' produce. They conduct schools and provide over 1500 scientific agricultural experts. They conduct over 4000 stations for seed selection, 8000 machine renting stations and rent out many thousands of tractors.

The more than 19,948 Handicraft cooperatives enrolled 1,760,000 members in 1930. They supply raw materials and market the product of the handicraft members, to whom the government renders every possible assistance. They also

---

[1] The Centrosoyus of the Consumers organizations maintains 58 traveling instructors and 2,336 connected with the local unions, with 75 educational institutions attended by over 9,500 students. They publish a central organ and many local newspapers, magazines, periodicals and bulletins. Over ten million dollars a year is appropriated for their cultural work. It would require a small volume adequately to describe it.

publish papers, magazines, books and pamphlets. Altogether the cooperatives play an increasingly important rôle in the socialization of both peasant and artisan labor. They are helping to develop the cooperative spirit in the whole Russian people.

Foreign Trade and Russian Dumping

The centralization of foreign trade in the hands of the government gives Russia a capacity for bulk export which creates a very significant situation in many industries. Russia, with her immense reserves of oil, has shown her power to undersell in the petrol markets. She could do the same in timber, woodpulp and matches from her enormous resources. The harvest of 1930 made her a factor by her export of grain to many countries. And it must be remembered that she is only at the beginning of a vast process of the mechanization and industrialization of agriculture where her resources and her unity of action are alike incomparable. In Germany the cartels have shown something of the efficiency of centralized purchase and sale. The British Dominions have created valuable export boards and Great Britain is about to do the same with coal. Japan's government action in the cotton trade has already been disastrous for Lancashire; indeed her foreign trade is today probably more than double what it would have been without the effective aid and support of the government. But all these are piecemeal and fractional compared with the Soviets' growing power.

This centralized control in Russia gives to each individual trade the advantage of dealing with the world as a whole as customer or buyer, and it links up the commercial tactics of one trade with others. There is always danger in bureaucracy but there is also strength in unity. This gives Russia a power possessed by no other country. It may be brought to bear for or against any country as an economic weapon.

America and Europe have been much exercised over the alleged dumping of Russian products at prices so low that they are said to menace both the farmer and manufacturer. As Russian exports are likely to increase during the next decade it may be useful to consider the real facts of the case.

Several things must be borne in mind before hastily judging regarding dumping. In the first place we must not swallow too credulously either Russian propaganda or counter propaganda which is often not only alarmist but bitter and prejudiced. We must remember that dumping is no new thing. It finds a recognized place in the Encyclopædia Britannica. For the last decade or two American dumping has been the complaint of Europe. Dumping has its ominous side for certain trades which may suffer thereby, but on the other hand anything that decreases the cost of grain and of bread may also benefit the consumer.

The outbreak of dumping at a time when the world market was in the worst possible state to absorb forced sales can only be attributed to the urgency of Russia's capital requirements. An objective consideration of the actual facts of Russian trade would hardly give ground for alarm.

Russia is not a great trading nation like the United States, for her entire foreign trade amounts to less than two per cent of the world's total. Her total exports to the United States are far exceeded by her purchases here. For the Soviet fiscal year in 1930, while her sales in the United States were only $32,000,000, her purchases aggregated $145,000,000. During the six months period when Russia was accused of dumping, her purchases in the United States were more than six and one-half times her exports. During the first half of 1930 the Soviet Union was the sixth best foreign customer of the United States, while in the preceding year her rating was only sixteenth. During Russia's fiscal year ending September 30, 1930, the increase of her trade balance in favor of America was thirty to one.[1]

Russia is accused of dumping "huge quantities" of grain, coal, lumber, pulpwood, manganese and other commodities which are said to demoralize American industry. At one and the same time stories are circulated of Russia's complete collapse and of her prodigious dumping. Compared to her pre-war grain exports, averaging annually about eleven million tons, her exports during the past year have been less than a third of this amount. Throughout the summer the Soviet press gave accurate official reports of the progress of the crop.

The operations in wheat in question were conducted by the All-Russian Textile Syndicate on the Chicago grain market on September 9, 10 and 11, 1930. The total amount

---

[1] During the year ending September 30, 1930, Russia's exports increased $1,250,000 and her imports $37,350,000 over the preceding year.

of the sales was only 7,765,000 bushels out of 180,000,000 bushels sold. Canada had been hedging or selling futures to protect its own wheat stocks against the possible decline in prices due to the huge over-supply of the world. As Edward Jerome Dies says in his *Wheat Pit:* "Hedging is simply another form of insurance. It is a commercial price insurance which protects the owner of grain against price fluctuations. It makes dealing in actual grain a safe business." The price of wheat, with many other commodities, had been declining progressively for more than a year. The All-Russian Textile Syndicate would be the last to desire to lower the price. While the Syndicate sold wheat futures for less than $7,000,000 it has purchased in America $262,000,000 worth of cotton, $5,000,000 worth of sugar and $2,500,000 worth of machinery, which has been beneficial to American trade and to the American farmer.

The Bulletin of the National City Bank says: "Everybody seems to have forgotten that only a few weeks ago charges were made that the Canadians were selling short on the Chicago market. The truth about it all is that Chicago is the greatest hedging market for wheat in the world. . . . Hedging operations on the Chicago market seldom contemplate the shipment of wheat to Chicago. . . . This is the season of the year when the Russian government is acquiring grain from its State farms or the peasant growers. It may desire to hedge its holdings promptly, as protection against a decline. . . . Hedge sales on the Chicago market in anticipation of actual distribution would be following the usual practice in the grain trade. . . . Short selling like any contract engagement is an act of business judgment. Since sales and purchases are being made by many persons and form a continuous stream of business there is no reason for doubting that on the whole they practically offset and cancel each other. On the whole they are beneficial to producers as broadening the market.

"It cannot be doubted that the publicity given to the Russian short sales and importance attributed to them have exerted an unfavorable influence upon wheat prices. It is interesting to note that among the advocates of extreme measures to prevent the 'dumping' of foreign wheat in the United States are the leading advocates of the various proposals for 'dumping' American products on foreign markets, as embodied in the McNary-Haugen Bill and the export debenture proposition. . . . We confess to skepticism toward representations that under these circumstances they deliberately and designedly sell their products for less than they might obtain. . . . We doubt that they intend to enrich the capitalist countries by giving something for nothing or on any better terms than seem to be necessary. They are wanting goods which they cannot produce and are striving to get them by the only means available to them. Nor are we very much alarmed about what they may do when they have developed their organization and become strong, efficient and well-equipped."[1]

Likewise the "huge" American imports of Soviet coal amounted to approximately one-tenth of one per cent of the

---

[1] *Bulletin of the National City Bank,* October, 1930.

American production. They consisted of special grade anthracite which is sold to the American distributor at a figure above the American price.[1]

American imports of timber and pulpwood from Russia were only one per cent of our total imports of these products and one-tenth of one per cent of the value of mill cut timber in the United States.[2] American paper mills have to import over 50 per cent of their supply of pulpwood and are in danger of a possible Canadian monopoly. Soviet pulpwood imports have been small in quantity and often command a higher price than Canadian pulpwood, but they tend to break the monopoly and lower prices for the American consumer.

In manganese ore, which has long been required by the American steel industry, the Russian Chiaturi fields have been a major source of supply for half a century. American mines are only able to furnish some 6.95 per cent of the required supply while Russia has furnished 47 per cent in spite of the duty which amounts to some 74 per cent. Soviet ore, far from being dumped, commands a high price. A

---

[1] Soviet anthracite of special grade is sold in Boston at more than $2.00 per ton above the mine price of American anthracite. The total production of coal in the United States is over 600,000,000 tons, of anthracite 76,640,000. The imports from Russia during the year according to our Department of Commerce were only 113,170 tons. Russian miners receive a money wage of 36 cents an hour, those in Great Britain 28 cents an hour. Allowing for the value of social services, insurance, etc., Russian miners receive 54 cents an hour compared to 31.5 cents for British miners.

[2] Department of Commerce figures for 1929 were $872,217 for imports of wood and manufactures therefrom. The United States produces little spruce and imported spruce sells at 30 per cent higher than our own domestic soft woods.

similar situation is found in imports of matches and candy from Russia.

Stories have been successfully circulated in America that imports of lumber, pulpwood, etc., were the product of convict or forced labor. Workers in Russia are normally employed through public employment exchanges in which labor organizations have a direct voice. Seasonally peasants are employed in winter in the northern forests scattered over hundreds of miles and along rivers. Such scattered units could not successfully be composed of convicts. The total number of all convicts in Russia engaged in labor is very small, less than one per cent of Russia's working force. For the small fraction of her export trade she has no need to employ convict labor. Reputable American importers who have visited the industries from which imports are derived have described the labor conditions in affidavits and denied the use of convict labor. Nearly a thousand American engineers and technicians in Russia are witnesses of their methods.

Unfortunately there are many who do not really desire to know the facts in the case. Wild rumors and false fears have a way of obtaining strange credence as in the case of our being victimized by our own propaganda concerning the Germans in wartime. Like a superhuman personal devil the Germans were everywhere, they could do anything, they commanded unlimited sums of money. There is the same amazing appeal to fear and credulity today regarding Russia. A few interested persons by a little carefully directed propaganda can make an effective appeal to prejudice and an approach to wartime hysteria.

The writer wishes to bear personal testimony that, apart from the handling under the G. P. U. of political and religious prisoners which he has elsewhere described and condemned, the Russian penal system on the whole is probably the most modern, rational and humane of any in the world. The entire plan is based not on the vindictive but upon the redemptive principle. In view of the open disgrace of many American prisons and their crying need of reform it would appear almost hypocritical for Americans to raise an outcry against prison labor in Russia. It would, however, be well worth while if it could eventually lead to the appointment of a commission which, after making a thorough study of conditions of prisons and of convict labor in Russia, could make a comparative study of the penal system of the United States with a view to the introduction of sweeping and much-needed reforms in this country.

Such a commission is the last thing that many would wish. It is easier to launch a series of attacks based on clumsy "documents" of unknown origin,[1] like the forged Zinoviev letter against the MacDonald Government or those connected with the alleged nationalization of women to which we shall refer later.

---

[1] Some have purported to show that the Amtorg Trading Corporation was fomenting political conspiracies in the United States and spreading "propaganda." According to these reports officers of Amtorg were engaged in smuggling into the United States Swiss watch movements valued at less than $1,000, while hazarding the ruin of their legitimate business of $150,000,000 a year.

CHAPTER V

Through this remarkable triumvirate of the Communist Party, the Soviet Government, as the first Communist world state, and the Comintern or Third International, the dictatorship of the organized proletariat, proposes to extend its sway in widening circles from an inner, all-powerful, dominating group, to the final anticipated regime of a world communist society. As stated in its Constitution: "The directive principle of the organizational structure of the Party is *democratic centralization*." Behind this word "democratic" there is in theory the will of the growingly organized and articulate proletarian workers, and in practice the delegated power of the organized Communist Party of Russia, now numbering, with its probationers, 1,852,090.[1] Below these Party members are the 2,466,000 Komsomols, or senior members of the Youth Movement, and 3,301,458 Pioneers and Octobrists, or junior members, which with the trade unions will furnish the majority of recruits prepared for future membership in the Party. The periodic "cleansings" of this body, like the annual pruning of a vine, are designed to keep the Party small and limit its numbers to a

---

[1] Statistics furnished by Statistical Department of the Gosplan, August, 1930. Of these a little more than 1,200,000 are full members and over 600,000 are candidates.

really vital, working, loyal membership, continually purged of dead wood.[1]

At its base the Party begins with a nucleus or cell in each village, factory, or organization wherever there are three or more members, and from its 50,000 local branches leads up to a highly centralized directive center, or political bureau. Thus the "voluntary centralism" of the Party focusses power in a very small group. There are nine full members of the inner, all-powerful political bureau, dominant among whom is Stalin, Secretary General of the Communist Party. This Party influences and largely dominates the Soviet Government of Russia, the trade unions and their world organization called the Profintern; and the Comintern or Third International. The whole plan lends itself to a powerful and effective centralization, yet also to constant touch with and the democratic discussion of the masses. Most questions may be referred to the rank and file for decision. Before every congress there is a thorough debate leading down to every cell and soviet group in Russia.

In the whole organization the individual matters little; the cause, the workers of the world and the Revolution, all represented by the Party, are everything. The individual seems almost a cipher until the social unit of the Revolution and its organization are placed before him and give him significance. There is a close parallel between the constitution

---

[1] The first article of the Constitution of the Communist Party reads: "Everyone who subscribes to the party program, works in one of its organizations, submits to party decisions and pays membership dues is considered a party member." Article I:1 of the Constitution adopted at the Fourteenth Congress of the Party in December, 1925.

of the Communists and the Jesuits. Each Jesuit owes strict and absolute obedience to his superior; while each communist individual and group, is responsible to the immediately superior organ of authority. Both organizations seem to believe that the end justifies the means and that the individual matters little compared to the great end of a common humanity, or the elect class of it that is to them significant. Both may be flamingly intolerant, both dogmatic, but none can question the intelligence or earnestness of either.

To understand how the communists were able to achieve such a powerful central control, coupled with such a wide base of democratic discussion and organization of the workers and peasants, we must recall their history. Radical ideas from foreign countries began to spread among the student class in Russia in the sixties of the last century, but the intellectuals were unable to touch the individualistic peasants. After 1872 the first small groups of organized workers marked the beginning of a labor movement in Russia, but it was later savagely suppressed by the Czarist police. In 1898 a group of nine men representing six organizations organized the Russian Social Democratic Labor Party. Lenin devised a plan for centralized control and in 1900 organized a workers' party paper called *Iskra,* the *Spark,* which kindled leaders of local groups of revolutionaries throughout Russia, and later throughout Europe when many of them were exiled.[1]

---

[1] The early program covered fourteen points including "self-determination for all peoples, separation of the church from the state and the school from the church, the eight-hour day, and a legislative organ composed

When a break in the party occurred Lenin led the majority, or "Bolshevik," section, demanding strict centralization and an uncompromising Marxian program of the dictatorship of the proletarian workers, refusing to cooperate with the bourgeois Liberals as advocated by the Menshevik, or minority section.[1] At the second revolution of November 7, 1917, this small, resolute party became the new rulers of Russia. Some of them believed they could not remain in power for six months and it looked for a long time as if the government could not endure. Allied intervention, however, consolidated all loyal elements in the defense of Russia against foreign invasion, and a policy of sagacity and force led to the establishment of what is now, apparently, one of the strongest and most stable governments in the world.

---

[1] The first struggle for power came in 1905 after the defeat of the Japanese war when on "bloody Sunday" the workers were shot down before the Czar's palace. Without a strong middle class in Russia and unsupported by the peasants and the army the revolt of the workers failed and a period of merciless reaction set in. From this time the movement was driven underground and the revolutionary leaders divided their time between prison and exile in Russia, and activities throughout the capitals of Europe, with a dwindling party reduced finally to a handful of resolute leaders. In 1905 the party had claimed three million adherents, in 1906 one million, in 1907 three-quarters of a million, in 1908 174,000, in 1910 46,000. Yet seven years later, in the name of all workers, peasants and soldiers, a group of not over a hundred fearless leaders seized the government of the largest undivided empire in the world. The provisional government was overthrown by the Petrograd Soviet of workers, which handed over power to the second all-Russian congress of Soviets. There were at this time some 50,000 members of the party. *Soviet Rule in Russia*, p. 695.

---

of representatives of the people." It concluded: "the necessary condition of the social revolution is the dictatorship of the proletariat, that is, the gaining by the latter of such political authority as would permit it to suppress any opposition by the exploiters." *Soviet Rule in Russia*, p. 691.

In 1923 the name Russia was dropped and the U. S. S. R., or Union of Socialist Soviet Republics was adopted, in which Russia proper becomes only one of a nucleus of autonomous republics, to which other countries may be added later in this proposed world organization.[1] The organization of the Communist Party is closely parallel to that of the Soviet Government itself. The unwieldy congress of the Party and its central committee are further centralized in its two powerful sub-committees for political and organizing activity in the political bureau of nine full members;[2] an organization bureau of twelve full members, with a secretariat of five;[3] Stalin as Secretary General is a member of each, with a small group of interlocking directors. His power is enormous. He is the chief of the paid Party

---

[1] At the same time the name of the party was changed to the "All-Union Communist Party." At the time of the Revolution two-thirds of the members of the Party were workmen, nearly a third were from the intelligentsia and salaried workers, and only 7.6 per cent were peasants. By 1928 there were 60.5 per cent workers, 19.2 per cent peasants and 19.7 per cent were employees and others. Of these 73.2 per cent are in towns and 26.8 per cent in the villages. Among the adult population about 1.35 per cent belong to the Communist Party.

[2] Lenin stated at the Ninth Party Congress in 1921: "All questions of domestic and foreign policy were settled by the polit-bureau," Report of Ninth Congress, p. 90. There is also a central revision committee and a central control commission to secure for the Party "actual supervision over the state and economic organs."

[3] Theoretically the supreme organ of the Party is the all-Union congress which usually adopts reports prepared in advance by the inner groups, as is the case also in regional areas. The same is probably true of most political parties in the world. In the interim between congresses a central committee of 71 members and 50 candidates is supreme. The Constitution of the Party reads: "The central committee organizes for political work a polit-bureau, for general administrative organization work an org-bureau, and for the current work of organization and execution a secretariat." Constitution, Section IV: Article 26.

workers throughout the country. He is in close touch with the Party organizations and can reward his followers or penalize his enemies. He may promote or demote the principal officials. He may exile or banish his enemies like Trotzky. But above all he must know in advance what policies will be approved by the supreme bodies in authority and by the workers and peasants of the country as a whole. He must always keep a majority of the Party behind him. Herein lies his power, and also the check or guarantee that he shall not individually misuse his power.

By sagacity rather than by force the Communist Party is everywhere in real control. Thus Stalin speaks of the Party as the "helm of the government." [1] To imagine its power think of one political party in the United States which should include practically all who have or desire to have the gift of leadership in political, industrial or social life. Include all leaders in politics, chambers of commerce, women's organizations, labor unions and even student and youth organizations. Organize this party into a widely democratic body for discussion and the discovery and creation of public opinion, yet as a highly centralized body for effective execution, after policies have been agreed upon by a majority

---

[1] Fifteenth Party Congress, 1927. Zinoviev declared at the Twelfth Congress that the real dictatorship was that of the Party while the Soviet Government was but the fifth wheel. He said: "The central committee of the party is in fact not only the central committee of the party but also of the soviets, of the trade unions, of the co-operatives, and of the entire workers' class. Therein lies its principal rôle; therein the dictatorship of the party is expressed." *Stenographic Report of the Twelfth Congress*, p. 207. Batsell, p. 709. Stalin and other communists would not agree that the Government is a fifth wheel.

in any supreme organ of authority.   Make this the one and only legally permitted Party; place its members in every important office, position and strategic locality, and you will have some conception of the position and power of the Communist Party in Russia.

Let us always remember also that this organization is not in the midst of a highly developed, cultured, politically minded, western democracy with long traditions of dearly bought liberty.   It rules among a backward, undeveloped, primitive, agricultural, semi-oriental people, accustomed to centuries of tyranny, where life can be simplified, standardized, organized and unified to a degree that would be impossible and inconceivable in western Europe or America. Apart from a few leaders the best communist, like the best soldier, is unthinking and obedient.   Among such a people life has been repeatedly simplified and unified by some great movement like Islam in Asia.   It is this failure to realize the total dissimilarity of Russia to the democratic countries that leads the West erroneously to think that such a dictatorship cannot possibly endure, and causes the leaders of Russia to envisage a speedy revolution in other lands.   The two are poles apart in mutual misunderstanding.

The Communist Party ramified in thousands of cells in factories, villages, trade unions, cooperatives, etc., seeks to guide and direct all these organizations in the interests of the workers and peasants themselves.   They have the best minds, the practical education, the experience, and the political, economic and financial power to make their program effective.   The policies of a political boss, or gang, or corrupt political ring are usually selfish, to exploit the masses for their own power and profit. But this Party, always of, for and by the workers, however great its centralization, sternly eliminates personal, private profit and punishes with death the grafter who betrays the workers and their cause. In this spirit the policy of domination is quite frankly acknowledged.[1]

In reality, as we have seen, the most influential governing body in the Party and in all Russia, is not the unwieldy congress or Central Committee, but the inner group of the political bureau, composed of nine members and eight alternates, which meets constantly, whose decisions are binding for the Party, and which largely determines the policies of the government, the trade union movement and the Third International. It may help to visualize it to draw a triangle with the political bureau and the Communist Party at the apex, one line of influence extending to the Soviet Govern-

---

[1] Stalin says: "No important political or organizational problem is ever decided by our soviets and other mass organizations without directives from the Party. In this sense we may say that the dictatorship of the proletariat is, substantially, the 'dictatorship' of its vanguard, the 'dictatorship' of its Party, as the force which guides the proletariat." *Leninism,* p. 33. He says also: "To all responsible positions in the Government the Communist Party tries to nominate its candidates, and in 95 out of 100 cases those candidates are elected. Naturally, these candidates will follow out the theories of Communism in which they believe, and the directions of the Party. Therefore, a direct Communist leadership results . . . Here in Russia the Party openly admits that it does guide and give general direction to the government." *Soviet Russia in the Second Decade,* p. 153. Party members are concentrated in positions of strategic importance. In the village soviets 90.6 per cent of the members are non-party. In the Central Executive Committee only 35 per cent are non-party, while on the management of the government trusts only about 25 per cent are not members of the Party.

ment and the other to the Third International.   The political bureau is the super-General Staff with full power.

The Government of Russia.

A soviet is simply a committee.   The soviet system was not created by the Communist Party.   It came into existence as a series of emergency strike committees organized in factories and the army in 1905.   Though suppressed at the time, they were revived just before the Revolution, and "all power to the soviets" became the rallying cry of the Communists.   It became the organizational committee system of the new "Workers and Peasants Government."   Everyone in Russia who is above eighteen years of age has the right to vote except the disfranchised who constitute a little over 5 per cent of the adult population.   Representation in the soviets or councils is occupational rather than territorial. Each factory, organization, city or village has its soviet or committee.

Just as the organization of the Party rises in a kind of step pyramid from the democratic base which includes all the members, to the highest block of the political bureau and the secretariat, so the Soviet Government has a parallel organization.   The supreme organ of authority at the base of the pyramid which is supposed to represent all workers and peasants is the All-Union Congress of Soviets, with some 1500 members, which meets at least once in two years. During the interval between congresses the supreme authority devolves upon the Central Executive Committee which would correspond in other countries to the two houses of a legislature. The Council of the Union, of 371 members, is elected by the Congress from representatives of the seven constituent republics which now make up the U. S. S. R. The Council of Nationalities, of 139 members, is formed of delegates from each of the autonomous republics and regions. This Central Executive with its two houses determines the general principles of the political and economic policy of the U. S. S. R. Between the sessions of this Central Executive Committee its Presidium of 21 members is the supreme legislative, executive and administrative organ of authority. The Council of People's Commissaries, is the executive and directive organ of the Central Executive Committee.[1]

Another legal division of the government provided for by the Constitution is the G. P. U., an abbreviation for State Political Department.[2] This is a secret service designed to combat counter-revolution and economic espionage and sabotage. In the early days of the revolution an Extraordinary Commission called the Cheka was formed. Its reputation was as unsavory as that of the similar tribunal during the terror of the French Revolution.[3] The Cheka

---

[1] It includes the Commissary for Agriculture, Finance, Labor, Interior, Justice, Workmen's and Peasants' Inspection, Education, Health, and Social Welfare. It is composed of 12 members and is similar to a cabinet in other countries but has even more power. It can pass emergency legislation subject to the later approval of the Central Executive Committee.

[2] After the formation of the U. S. S. R. in 1923 the word "unified" was added, making the Russian form O. G. P. U.

[3] *Martov at the Seventh Congress of Soviets* in 1919 declared that it had become an "omnipotent authority of the organs of oppressing and

with its odium and fear was abolished in 1922 and the more restricted and constitutional G. P. U. substituted. With all its restrictions it is still probably the most powerful and dreaded police organization in the world. Stalin describes it as "the punitive organ of the soviet power, resembling the Comité de Salut Publique of the French Revolution. It represents something like a military-political tribunal, constituted to protect the revolution against the assaults of the counter-revolutionary bourgeoisie and its agents." The G. P. U. has its own separate armed force, its own prisons and its own secret courts. It has the right to arrest any one but must notify the attorney general of the Supreme Court within forty-eight hours, and must try the case within one month. In the special G. P. U. courts the accused is not allowed counsel, nor is he permitted to call witnesses in his own defense.[1] He is given a trial but it is secret.

The G. P. U. is an agency of "class justice." It can best be understood under the conditions of a war psychosis such as prevailed during and after the French Revolution when

---

[1] The accused has the right of appeal to the attorney general or the Presidium, and a second appeal to the Central Executive Committee. In 1922 to 1927 some 1500 were said to have been executed by the G. P. U., or an average of 300 per year. There were probably many more, but there is no way of checking the action of an unknown and dreaded secret tribunal by democratic process, nor is it subject to public opinion.

---

police administration. . . . The government was forced completely to surrender before the Cheka, placing at its will the life, liberty and honor of the citizens. The monstrous growth of the terror, the elimination of everything which resembled courts, and an uncontrolled rule of anarchy are the results of this policy." *Soviet Rule in Russia*, p. 482.

its leaders feared their ancient foe of Bourbon oppression, and believed that they were fighting for social justice with the rest of the world against them. It can also be understood by the same war hysteria when the United States Government under Attorney General Palmer issued warrants for the arrest of 6,500 aliens, and used *agents provocateurs* in hunting them. Even former Secretary of State Hughes admits this action "savored of the worst practices of tyranny."

It is obvious that the Soviet state has the same right to protect itself against sedition as any other. It will probably be found on careful study that its *public* penal system is one of the most advanced, the most modern and redemptive in the world. Even certain reformatories and rehabilitation colonies for youth carried on by the G. P. U. are more scientific, more humane and successful than any that we know in any other country. Yet when the treatment of the old *intelligentsia* is remembered, some of them once the revolutionary leaders of Russia, when the practice of the secret courts of the G. P. U. dealing with political and religious prisoners is realized, no analogies, no explanation, no excuses will win the approval of the democratic world with its hardwon toleration and civil liberties, until this medieval agency of class justice, and sometimes of injustice, is brought out into the open light of day as among more advanced, civilized nations. A terror may subjugate Russia and be tolerated by the unthinking mass under the centralized few, but so long as it continues it wins the odium of the world.

The Red Army and Navy have enrolled 562,000 officers

and men since 1924.[1] The Red Army is a class weapon for the defense of the proletarian revolution. It is a conscript body from the working classes, 75 per cent peasants and 15 per cent workers, but excludes all non-proletarian elements which might not be in sympathy with the aims of the government. It places as much emphasis upon training in literacy and political ideology for communist citizenship as it does upon military drill. It is a far more loyal and efficient fighting force than the old army of the autocratic Czars. It is manifestly a defensive army in keeping with the Soviet's whole international policy. It has a strong infantry and a good cavalry complement, but it is weak in artillery, transport, aviation and in all technical branches. The navy is negligible, being inferior even to that of Germany or Spain.

The Soviet Union is pouring its whole strength into economic rather than military development. As you see those tow-headed country boys in uniform in Russia, they are the least military looking of any army in Europe. It is an army that would be strong in retreat, but neither adequately equipped nor trained for strong offensive warfare. They could fall back before an invading army some six thousand

---

[1] The official strength of the Soviet army has been as follows:

1920	3,538,000
1921	4,110,000
1922	1,590,000
1923	703,000
1924	562,000

The Czarist army in peace-time strength numbered in 1913, 1,200,000, in 1914, 1,800,000. *The Soviets in World Affairs,* by Louis Fischer, Vol. II, p. 758.

miles if necessary, and then march back and recapture their lost territory as they did with Napoleon's retreating and decimated forces. There would be no more hope of invading and conquering Russia, than the United States or Canada. Each would probably prove ultimately invulnerable to such military attack.

An offensive military invasion by Soviet Russia for imperialistic conquest would be a contradiction to the whole Marxian system, but not only the army but wellnigh the whole people would again rally to the defense of the Government in the face of foreign invasion or intervention, accompanied by cruel and stupid atrocities that such a class war would inevitably call forth, as in 1918. Russian communists are averse to all international or imperialist wars, but they are not at all pacifistic. They believe in class war from within each country, where each nation shall follow the example of Russia itself when the time is ripe.

Russia is adequately armed for defense in accordance with her policy. A comparison with the military strength of neighboring nations and of the industrial program of these nations shows where Russia is placing her emphasis.[1] It is not in military but in economic strength.

	Population	Size of Army	Soldiers Per 1000 Inhabitants
France	40,743,000	673,000	16
Italy	42,000,000	353,000	8
Poland	29,589,000	270,000	9
Roumania	17,153,000	325,000	18
Soviet Union	160,000,000	562,000	3.5

[1] *Ibid*, p. 760. See *Europa Year Book*, London, and *World Almanac*, 1930, p. 231.

In the United States 72 per cent of the national budget is devoted to military or war purposes. In Russia 63 per cent of the revenue is devoted to industrialization, 21 per cent to education and cultural purposes, 10 per cent to administration and defence, and 6 per cent to remaining needs.[1]

The Third International.

The Communist or Third International was founded on the ruins of its two predecessors in 1919.[2] At present it unites the Communist Parties in 66 nations, some 40 in Europe, 20 in the Orient and the remainder in North and South America. The first Congress in Moscow with 60 delegates adopted frankly its constitution for the overthrow of capitalism and the setting up of soviet republics patterned upon that of Russia, looking toward a final world-wide International Soviet Republic to be established by means of world revolution. This frankly avowed policy is not denied by any responsible communist and is stated repeatedly in all their literature.

Article I of the Constitution reads: "The new International Workmen's Association is formed for the organization of joint action by the proletariats of various countries, who are struggling for the same aims: the overthrow of capitalism, the creation of a dictatorship of the proletariat

---

[1] *The Economist,* London, November 1, 1930.

[2] The first international was established by Marx in London, in 1864. It was dissolved in 1876 after the split between Marx and Bakunin. The second international was formed in 1889. In 1915 the socialists who opposed the war formed the nucleus of the new organization which, after the Russian Revolution of 1917, was finally organized in 1919. The second international of course remains in existence.

and an International Soviet Republic for the complete abolition of classes and the realization of Socialism, the first steps toward a Communist society."

The twenty-one points drafted by Lenin to indicate the duties of members of the Comintern or Third International are clear and uncompromising: 1. All propaganda must be genuinely communistic and agree with the program and decisions of the Comintern. 2. Reformist elements must be removed from the leadership of each labor movement and replaced by true communists. 3. The revolution must be prepared for as civil war approaches in every country. 4. Propaganda must be carried on in each national army. 5. Farmers and peasants must be prepared for the coming conflict. 6. Social pacifism must be unmasked and the revolutionary overthrow of capitalism anticipated. 7. There must be a clean break with all reformist or compromising policy. 8. Colonies and oppressed nations must be prepared for freedom. 9. Communist agitation must be carried on in every trade union movement. 10. The second, Amsterdam, "yellow" trade union international must be opposed. 11. Each member must subordinate his entire activities to the interests of the revolution. 12. Democratic centralization must control all parties. 13. Party cleansings must be frequent. 14. Every soviet republic must be supported by every party. 15. Each party must have a complete communist program in harmony with the Comintern. 16. All decisions of Comintern Congresses and the Executive Committee are binding upon all the parties. 17. Every party must openly bear its name. 18. Party press organs must print all Comintern official documents. 19. All parties must call special conventions and inform local organizations of Comintern Congress decisions. 20. Central committees must be unambiguously for the Comintern. 21. All party members who reject the above conditions adopted by the Comintern are to be expelled.[1] In the last World Congress in Moscow in 1928, 475 delegates representing 58 parties participated. The Executive Committee of 59 chooses a Presidium of 29 members, 13 of whom compose the Political Secretariat.

Like the Party, the Third International has its iron discipline and centralized control strongly resented by the majority of trade union leaders of other countries such as the British. Communists from other nations represented in the Comintern or Third International would prefer to have its center "at the front" in some other capital such as Berlin, but only in Russia is it secure and legally recognized. As the Russian Party contributes most of the funds it naturally has a decisive voice in the decisions of the Executive Committee.

Each communist in Russia pays 2 per cent of his income to the Party chest, and one quarter of any amount he receives above the monthly Party maximum of 225 roubles, or $112.50. The Communist Party of each country forwards a certain proportion of its funds to the Comintern. There is no evidence that it receives any financial support

---

[1] Theses of Lenin adopted by the Second Congress of Communist International, Moscow, 1920. *The Communist International,* No. 13, quoted by Batsell, p. 761.

from the Soviet Government; in a sense it does not need it.
The budget for 1927 was officially stated at $700,000, re-
ceived chiefly from the dues and contributions from member
parties.[1]

The three countries where revolution is looked for most
hopefully at present by Russian leaders are Germany, China
and Poland.   Unrest in Germany will depend upon the extent
to which her laboring class is reduced in its standard of
living to pay reparations.   India has its own political na-
tionalist movement of which the Communists make up but
a small and infinitesimal minority and have little influence.
China furnishes in its civil war, chaos, banditry, famine and
desperate economic need, the one country most ripe for
regional communist dictatorship.   It is in China also that the
germ of communism seems to be the most virulent and
violent, breaking out again and again into atrocities wherever communists, or local reds, or bandits gain control under
the cloak of "communism."

Many in capitalist countries have constantly and eagerly
predicted the early downfall of the Soviet Government;
while orthodox communists have hoped for speedy revolution in other lands.   Nowhere in Europe or North America,
however, does there seem to be any likelihood of the early
overthrow of the existing social order, whether in com-

---

[1] In 1927 the published administrative expenses were $297,529.52, while
$345,103.42 were devoted to subsidies of Party newspapers and litera-
ture in various counties and their cultural, educational and propaganda
work.   Special help is given to those parties which are counted illegal in
such countries as China and India, Poland, Hungary and the Balkans.
See *Pravda,* Communist Party official newspaper for July 22, 1928.

munist Russia or the capitalistic nations.   In both the wish
is father to the thought.   These two conflicting social orders,
are likely to exist side by side for a long time to come.

Parallel to the organization of the Comintern is the
Profintern or Red Trade Union International which has
claimed a membership of 13,862,209 members, 10,248,000
of whom are in Russia.[1]   This organization frankly aids
strikes in other countries.   During four years, 1924–1927,
they made contributions totalling at least $316,495.49 in
support of strikes in thirty countries, in addition to very
large sums to the British Miners Strike in 1926.[2]

------

[1] Other Communist Parties are reported to number, in Germany 125,000,
Czechoslovakia 138,000, China 75,000, France 56,000, Sweden 17,000,
the United States 14,000, Great Britain 7,000.   In most countries of
Europe they have their legally elected representatives in parliament.

[2] *International Trade Union Movement,* Moscow, 1928, pp. 82-91, quoted
in W. H. Chamberlin's excellent work, *Soviet Russia,* pp. 268-270.

As we go to press the statements of this chapter have been confirmed
by the dismissal of Rykov in December, 1930.   Thus Stalin, who holds
no office in the Soviet Government, but is all-powerful in the Party, is
able without difficulty to dismiss Rykov, the brilliant Prime Minister,
and to discipline the powerful trio of the "right deviation."   Rykov,
Bukharin and Tomsky remain members of the Communist Party Central Committee which is the supreme ruling body.   In recent years the
political bureau, however, has tended to become the supreme authority,
holding the position of a European Cabinet backed by a majority in
Parliament.

CHAPTER VI

EDUCATION AND CULTURE

As we have seen, Russia offers an example of the most complete and continuing revolution in history. There is a new literature, a new art and education, a new conception of society, of law, of morality, of religion—all seems new, even to the psychology and temperament of the people. In place of the fatalistic, casual, easy-going, undisciplined Slav, one now finds a release of energy, initiative and indomitable enterprise born of a crusading spirit. This has been strikingly manifest in the whole esthetic field. Unlike the Puritan, the communist has preserved and developed the artistic side of life. The revolution found a common expression in the political, economic and artistic fields. All were volcanic and bursting with energy. In Czarist days the repressed people, debarred from politics and undeveloped in economic life, found expression in the artistic sphere in literature, art and music. The new Russia, unrestrained, is expressing itself also in these fields.

In no other country, unless it be Japan, has the esthetic side of life been so fostered and developed among the common people. In no other country does one find the art galleries, the museums, the opera, concert and theatre, all of the highest quality, so thronged with working men. The huge art gallery of the Czar in Leningrad has been greatly

115

enlarged. The art collections from the palaces of the nobles, like the palaces themselves are now all socialized and made available to the people. The government's concern and the people's appreciation for them is equally commendable. No country has better preserved its treasures of art and archaeology. Even the churches and ecclesiastical structures in the Kremlin are being stripped of the vulgar modern coating of the later Czars and restored to their early classic beauty.

The new literature bears the impress of the revolution and expresses its psychology. It is prevailingly creative, realistic, naturalistic, full of self-criticism, though still often youthful, crude and unfinished. It is still passing through a transitional stage of experimentalism. The new proletarian poetry, bursting with revolutionary enthusiasm, and believing in the early triumph of the world revolution, expressed itself in songs of praise to labor, to the machine, to iron and steel, and titanic human muscles. It was naturally often materialistic and collectivist.

Art as well as literature voiced the revolution, at first in striking posters and cartoons which have been a powerful factor of propaganda for the common people. Art is conceived as the instrument for "the socialization of the emotions." Both art for art's sake, and art as a medium of propaganda are recognized in Russia. John Dewey was impressed by "the contrast between the popular notion of universal absorption in materialistic economy and the actual facts of devotion to the creation of living art and to universal participation in the processes and the products of art."

The revolution has transformed the Russian theatre. Politically restricted before the war, it was immediately flung wide open to the masses. Not only the brilliant naturalism of Stanislavsky's Art Theatre in Moscow and the genius of Meyerhold's revolutionary theatre appeal to the metropolitan population, but the strong dramatic instinct of the Russian character is expressed in the remotest villages. The Russian has a natural gift for and an almost religious consecration to the dramatic. The theatre touches him deeply. The villain of capitalism and the hero of communism play their parts in an infinite variety of settings on the Russian stage. Perhaps no other people could have so dramatized the revolution and could so embody it in art, in architecture, in sculpture, on the stage, in the motion picture and in literature. No other nation has made the cinema such an instrument of education, with such a powerful political and social message. Instead of a merely commercialized amusement and a social menace, it is made a vast educational force for teaching the socialized conceptions and building the kind of character they desire. Lenin had said that "of all our arts I believe that the cinema is the most important."

Even music has been made a medium of expression of the revolution, especially for the newly awakened racial minorities. The "International" was ready for adoption as the Soviet national hymn. At every large gathering or celebration among the Russians it takes the place of "God Save the King" for a British audience. The Youth Movement has its fresh songs and is finding dramatic and artistic expression, while workmen's songs have been produced in great numbers.

With the effort to eliminate religion, art in all its forms will probably find increasing expression and value in Soviet Russia. Its chief limitation and handicap is likely to be that of the narrowing, materialistic, utilitarian character of the dogma upon which the continuing revolution is based.

Education.

The new education is in striking contrast to the old. Two decades ago we found an educational system in Czarist Russia designed for the privileged classes.[1] Higher education was prevailingly cultural and individualistic, often romantic and apart from life. It frequently produced introverts of the Hamlet type. The new education is experimental, social, practical and utilitarian, producing a new psychological type of extroverts, with a tremendous release of enthusiasm, of creative energy, of courage and confidence in life. The old system was for a special class. The new is for an enlightened mass, a whole nation ultimately to be educated.

No country has a system of education that is a more unified whole, logically based upon a complete philosophy of life, vitally integrated and interwoven with the interests of the people. As Professor Paul Monroe of Columbia University observes: "Nowhere does this enthusiasm for and belief in an educational program so permeate every element

---

[1] Before the war the proportion of illiteracy among army recruits was among the French, 4 per cent, the British, one per cent, the Germans, one-twentieth of one per cent, the Russians, 62 per cent. In the latter country only 3.3 per cent of the entire population was in school. *Education in Soviet Russia*, p. 16.

in society and so control and direct the action of those in authority." [1]

The whole process is socialized. Based upon a consistent theory, the school is made responsible for instruction, but all life is harnessed in the process of practical education—the factory, the farm, the shop, the museum, the theatre and opera, the athletic field, the cooperative, the trade union, the home, the city and the village—all are brought to bear upon the education of youth. John Dewey speaks of the total situation in Russia as "an experiment by all means the most interesting one going on upon our globe." [2]

The old education aimed at the support of the Czarist *status quo* of church and state, the new seeks the creation of a cooperative commonwealth by the molding of youth and the re-education of a whole people upon a new principle of life. With one great social objective the system aims at a new economic order, the socialization of its political life, and the evolution of the culture of all the autonomous peoples of Russia in their own language and traditions. According to Lenin's widow, Krupskaia, the task of the present regime is "to enable every human being to obtain personal cultivation, to share to the fullest in all the things that give value to human life."

It is natural that all education in Russia should be under the control of the state for its consciously chosen ends. In

---

[1] "The history of education offers no parallel to the transformation that has been worked in the educational system of Russia," Prof. Counts in *The Culture Program of Soviet Russia* by Paul Monroe, p. 583, Carnegie Endowment Series, No. 255.

[2] *Impressions of Soviet Russia,* p. 114.

other countries education is often more unconsciously, while in Russia it is always consciously, propaganda. "Americanization" programs for foreigners and patriotic ceremonies connected with the flag have a legitimate end in the United States. In America children are taught reverence for the Constitution, in Russia for Communism. "In Russia the propaganda is in behalf of a burning public faith—the universal good of universal humanity. In consequence, propaganda is education and education is propaganda." [1] The Marxian system is basic everywhere. The teaching of science is frankly designed to make materialists of the children. An elaborate pre-school system seeks to develop creative activity and cooperative and collectivist habits. The nursery and the school probably play a larger part in the training of the children than does the home.

The central idea in Russian education is the "complex system." As society is conceived as a complex whole in which each individual functions socially, so the school should represent a cross section of this concrete life. It is held that the subject of instruction should not be some isolated academic topic like history or economics, nor some trivial project, but some actual whole situation or complex, such as

---

[1] John Dewey, *Impressions of Soviet Russia,* p. 56. Lenin writes: "The school, apart from politics, is a lie, a hypocrisy. Bourgeois society indulged in this lie, covering up the fact that it was using the schools as a means of domination, by declaring that the school was politically neutral, and in the service of all. We must declare openly what it concealed, namely the political function of the school. While the object of our previous struggle was to overthrow the bourgeoisie, the aim for the new generation is much more complex: it is to construct Communist society." Quoted by John Dewey in *Impressions of Soviet Russia,* p. 82.

sanitation, home economics, the school, village or city. They pass from life to knowledge, they seek to learn by doing. The excursion is an instrument. Nature, museums, shops and libraries are all classrooms for the study of life.

A new departure in the soviet school system aims to attach each school from the secondary grades to the university to some industrial, agricultural or other institution. Thus the factory and the farm are made a part of the school system, and the school becomes a part of the industrial system. It is a vital part of the national life. The old university has given place to a number of institutes and factory schools.

Another characteristic of Russian education is self-government, and the absence of external restriction from an early age. Discipline is maintained by democratic organizations of the students themselves. Pupils in lower grades have a degree of liberty corresponding to university students in other lands. The writer has met with high school students from rural districts who were studying in the nearest city under their own effective and complete self-government and self-imposed moral standards, with no older person in charge of them. The Russians believe that students taught to think for themselves can be trusted. In higher institutions the curriculum is determined by the joint representatives of the organized faculty and organized students, with the former in the majority. They are concerned not only with weeding out of the course students intellectually unfit for the work, but even more in eliminating faculty members incompetent to teach. Apart from the Marxian system, education is conceived not as something handed down by authority to be imposed upon the young, but as a joint sharing of experience by the older and younger generations in a democratic process. We shall deal in a later section with the Marxian dogma.

The Czarist Russian student organizations were ordinarily forbidden by the state. Today they are a vital part of the system of education. They organize for student activities such as sports or discipline, in their academic work, in economic cooperatives or trade unions, and in political youth organizations. All are training grounds in citizenship. One can hardly find an institution where students do not take part in the management or administration of the institution or of its activities. This is bound to have a bearing on the democratization of the future Russian state. An ultimate tyranny would not dare to educate its youth, workers and peasants in self-government. Whatever its object there is a vast process of democratization going on in Russia today which may determine its future.

There are no barriers of race but there are of class in a system conceived as a proletarian instrument. Dr. Jowett once thought of Balliol College, Oxford, as designed to teach an English gentleman to become an English gentleman. In contrast to this, the motto appearing over the entrance to Moscow University is "Science—for the Toilers."

The rabfacs, or workers' high schools, provide a short, practical course, usually of three years, which prepares the most promising of the young workers for the universities. From the 68,000 students in these full-time workers' day schools and night schools, more than a third of the students are drawn who enter the universities. Where the manual worker was formerly practically excluded, now the whole process of education, as far as possible, is proletarianized. This tends to dilute and lower the intellectual cultural standards of the universities, but also educates and provides leaders for the whole working mass. The Party plans that 65 per cent of the engineering students shall be drawn from the workshops and the working class.[1]

Education, like most things in Russia, is hampered by lack of funds. It receives about 10.6 per cent of the entire government budget as compared to 18.7 per cent in the United States.[2] According to the five-year plan, compulsory school attendance is to be required by 1931 and $1,750,-000,000 will be necessary to introduce it. Russia is fond of the challenge of ideals for the moment impossible.

The achievements of the Soviet system of education during the last decade are remarkable. There were but 4,400,000 in attendance in all schools in 1923. By 1930 the number of institutions and their total enrollment was as follows:[3]

---

[1] Bukharin writes: "The true basis and meaning of the dictatorship of the proletariat must be a proletarian monopoly of education. This may appear shocking, but the monopoly of education always was and always is the most important privilege of every ruling class. There is nothing else on which a ruling class can base its power. The monopoly of education must become the privilege of the proletariat if the proletariat is to win." *A B C of Communism*, p. 241.

[2] Figures for 1926-7 in Russia and 1925 in U. S. A. *Soviet Russia*, p. 295. In 1928-29, $639,500,000 were spent on education in the U. S. S. R., compared to $2,026,308,190 in the U. S. A. *Soviet Year Book*, 1930, p. 463 and *World Almanac*, 1930, p. 449.

[3] Figures furnished by *Statistical Department of the Gosplan*, August, 1930.

Class of Education	Institutions	Pupils
Elementary	129,660	12,320,928
Secondary	1,883	1,088,813
Professional	835	966,581
Rabfacs	239	68,185
Colleges	188	204,513
Schools for the Illiterate	168,800	6,112,078
Adult Education	2,152	210,532
Party Schools	112	17,061
Workers' Universities	88	32,058
Political and Party Education	44,811	1,015,050
Libraries	25,506	
Cottage Reading Rooms	20,068	
Clubs	4,752	
People's and Peasants' Homes	6,819	
Red Corners	48,661	
Theatres	1,434	
Cinemas	7,963	

In Czarist Russia in 1913, 40 per cent of the people were literate. Today, 68.9 per cent of those from sixteen to thirty-four years of age are literate, and 27.5 per cent of those over fifty can read and write. Their strenuous program aims at the goal of the elimination of illiteracy by 1934, while in Russia proper a law has been passed requiring compulsory education for children from eight to eleven years of age.

Such truly titanic achievements must not blind us however to the defects in this system of education from an American point of view. There are now twenty million illiterates in Russia proper, while plant, equipment and teachers are still lacking for a third of the children. Universities are still unable to accommodate half the applicants for admission. Teachers are poorly paid, receiving an average salary of $26.87 a month in the elementary schools.

Education is practical, but scholastic standards have been lowered. The penalizing of not only the intelligentsia and the disfranchised, but their innocent children, has been condemned by the bolder and more tolerant leaders like Maxim Gorky and Krupskaia.[1] The worst feature of the system is the deliberately hostile propaganda maintained in schools and press, representing, or frequently misrepresenting, the worst features in the life of foreign peoples.[2] Insofar as there is the persistent cultivation of fear, bitterness and hatred, often by plain falsehood, it cannot commend itself to free and tolerant peoples. It must, of course, be admitted that this has been paralleled by a campaign of misrepresentation and falsehood in the press of other lands. It is to be hoped, however, that this unworthy feature of both systems may be eliminated, especially in a country that has already made such a brilliant and commendable educational advance as the Soviet Union.

---

[1] In 1928 out of 20,865 students admitted to universities in Russia proper 41.6 per cent were children of workers, 26.5 per cent of peasants, 11.3 per cent of the intelligentsia, 19.1 per cent of employees, 1.5 per cent of others. Chamberlin, *Soviet Russia*, p. 283.

[2] Bukharin writes: "Communist propaganda has become a necessity for the whole society now undergoing regeneration . . . It is therefore necessary that not merely the proletarian school but in addition the whole mechanism of the proletarian State should contribute to the work of communist propaganda. This propaganda must be carried on in the army; it must be carried on in and by all the instruments of the Soviet Power." *A B C of Communism*, p. 254.

CHAPTER VII

MORALS AND MARRIAGE

Moral standards of the new Russia are neither ascetic nor licentious. The *mores* or customs of the group are not conceived as absolute standards of divine authority, nor on the other hand is conduct viewed as a mere matter of individual concern or of self-gratification. Communists start with no eternal moral truths but with the authority of a social control which must rationally work out its norm of conduct, leaving the utmost freedom to the individual consistent with social welfare. Not the state as it exists today, but the classless society of the future is the norm. All that aids this revolutionary ideal is right, all that hinders it is wrong. Thus Lenin defined communist morality as "everything that will unite the workers against every form of exploitation, and serve to raise human society to a higher level." [1]

There is a very real danger in the new Russia that the

---

[1] Lenin says: "Certainly thirst must be satisfied, but does a normal person, under normal conditions, lie in the street and drink from mud puddles? Or even from a glass that dozens of other people have been drinking from? But still more important is the social aspect of it. Drinking water is an individual matter. But two participate in love and from it arises a third new life. Here the interests of society come in ... The revolution demands concentration; the straining of all energies by the masses and the individual. The proletarian is an advancing class. He doesn't need drunkenness to deaden or arouse him, either through sexual intemperance or alcohol. He needs clarity." *Woman in Social Russia,* p. 135.

individual may be absorbed in the mass, in "the collective man," and thus may not be able to make his full contribution to society. Experience will probably teach them that society can only be built with the help of more fully developed individuals.

Leading the way in the forming of moral standards are the youth organizations with their select, trained and strongly self-disciplined young people. For a short time after the Revolution there was a period of license when all restraint was counted "bourgeois," but today all promiscuity or sensuous indulgence or dissipation is counted "counter-revolutionary." The sex life of youth was lax five years ago. Today such laxity is discouraged or condemned, although the sex life of Russians is probably more free from constraint and interference than in any other country, and irregularity, whether among married or unmarried persons is less penalized. There are no "illegitimate" children, no "fallen" women, no sinful nor improper persons to be punished by moral condemnation or social isolation.

There is, however, a Communist Temperance Society and a vigorous campaign is carried on against drink and sexual excess. There is no smoking for Young Pioneers.[1] Among mature youth abstinence is to be practiced as far as possible, and where it is not, one permanent relationship is encouraged, whether registered or unregistered, rather than promiscuity. By absorption in hard work, by social service, preoccupation in vital interests, hardy athletics, mixed play

---

[1] One of the Pioneer rules reads: "The Pioneer watches out for his health and cleanliness, and neither smokes, nor drinks, nor swears."

and sensible fellowship between youth of both sexes, self-imposed moral standards are maintained with considerable success. Delinquencies are dealt with not as individual sin but as social betrayal.

Drink is a problem in Russia as in America. Vodka in Czarist days yielded about a quarter of the state revenue. Wartime prohibition was maintained through the early revolution, but it could not be continued in the face of widespread illicit peasant manufacture. Vodka was legalized in 1925, in full forty per cent strength, but the state manufacture and sale is only half the pre-war amount. The powerful propaganda posters, motion pictures and literature state that in Russia in 1927 the drink bill was 1,200,000,000 roubles, or $600,000,000, showing that this amount would have built 1,200,000 much needed homes, or provided 720,000 tractors in the elimination of backward agriculture. It is strange that democratic America is trying to solve its drink problem by force, while the autocratic dictatorship of Russia turns in this case to what they believe to be the more effective means of education and moral suasion. Neither however has as yet solved its problem.

There is an ascetic vein in Soviet Russia. Moscow looks like a bleak puritan city in comparison with the brilliantly lighted gaiety and night life of New York or Chicago. There is practically no public round dancing. The one poorly supported gambling house in Moscow has recently closed its doors. The two night clubs in the city, poorly attended, are largely a concession to foreigners and void of any sex attraction in entertainment such as would be found in New York, Paris or Berlin. There are no styles, no fashions to be maintained. All life has been levelled down to a drab and relatively equal standard of simplicity. A workman's clothes are in style in every place or at any entertainment. All seem poor together, but none appear destitute. Soviet Russia is serious. They seem happy in their recreation parks, especially in their games and folk dancing, but never frivolous, insolent or disorderly. "Cromwell and Milton would probably feel more at home in Moscow with its utter absence of gay night life, its contempt for frivolity, its intensive concentration on purposes far removed from individual enjoyment, in which respects it is strikingly different from the spirit which prevails in every other European capital." [1]

This puritan spirit comes as a surprise to the average American who visits Russia. On a recent tour conducted by the writer one member of the party gaily asked a beautiful young lady guide and interpreter, "Would you marry me?" "Certainly not," she replied frigidly. "Why, don't you ever joke about anything?" "Not about serious things," she said. "Then you regard marriage as a serious thing?" "Most certainly we do," she answered. When this same man was travelling from Moscow to Leningrad the porter of the sleeping car happened to enter his stateroom in the morning and found the American kissing his wife. The porter indignantly fined him twenty-five roubles, or $12.50.

---

[1] W. H. Chamberlin, *Soviet Russia,* p. 80. This book and Maurice Hindus' *Humanity Uprooted* probably give the truest pictures of life in Russia today in the English language.

It was no use for our friend to insist that the lady was his wife. It did not matter whose wife she was. The train inspector reinforced the porter's demand. The fine was paid under protest. Later the authorities called and returned the money with courteous apologies because the culprit was a foreigner; but no Russian would have been repaid. This chastened American formed a very different idea of prevailing moral standards from those opinions that he brought with him to Russia. Women when travelling in trains are especially protected.

Marriage and the Home.

The Revolution has affected marriage and the home as it has every other aspect of Russian life. In the chaos that followed the war and revolution there was a brief period of license and unrestraint manifest even more in Russia than in any other country. However, things never went to the lengths of the exaggerations and misrepresentations of foreign propaganda which persistently circulated such gratuitous lies as the nationalization of women.[1] Today a very definite code of marriage laws and a seriously self-disciplined youth movement frown upon all licentiousness and promiscuity.

In this as in every other regard the Soviet Union can

---

[1] Investigation shows that this was never done or even contemplated by the Communists at any time or place in Russia. In one centre, Saratov, just before an election, in 1918, there appeared an announcement purporting to come from their enemies and opponents, the Anarchists, proposing such a scheme locally. It was instantly repudiated even by the Anarchists as a forgery and a libel, and was never contemplated by the Communists whose whole conception of womanhood would have made it unthinkable.

only be understood in the light of its own background, rather than by comparison with western lands. Russia, whether old or new, was always free from the inhibitions, restraints and artificial repressions of other countries. Neither romantic feudalism nor stern puritanism had ever produced the aloofness and mystery connected with women, the artificial separation of the sexes, the morbid curiosity or dread of sex found in some other countries. Russian women were and probably are now the most sensible in the world. They are free, frank, serious, unfrivolous. They are neither afraid of sex nor preoccupied with it.

Sex is considered a wholesome thing but not an all-absorbing object in life. Russians are as a rule a vital, simple, unrepressed and uninhibited people. They are often amoral rather than immoral. There is an absence of sex suggestiveness in Russian life, literature and cinema. Sex intrigue is never the open or hidden lure in any motion picture. Not only would it be indignantly denounced but the people do not demand it. Sex is not taboo but is brought out rationally and critically into the open light of day. The result is probably a more natural and equal relation between the sexes in Russia than in any other country of the world.

Russia's old *Domostroy* book lays down some of the most savage customs under which women have ever been subjected to men. Man had complete authority over woman and was advised to use the rod freely to bring her under submission. The new code of laws, and much more the new spirit and conception of perfect equality for women, has completely swept away all the old man-made laws and customs of man's dominance, save where old habits still persist among the unsocialized portion of the peasantry.

The gist of the new moral code and practice is personal freedom based on social welfare. Complete liberty is granted both to men and women, but their action is always conditioned by social consequences. The law is relentless in enforcing responsibility for offspring. Therefore society discountenances intemperate self-gratification and demands judicious self-control. The weight of revolutionary public opinion is for social welfare, not individual license.

Marriage in Russia is regarded as a vital, personal relation between man and wife. Love makes marriage real. They conceive that the state cannot make or break marriage. It can only recognize or register the fact of it. It can protect children or guard society against the prostitution or perversion of it to selfish and antisocial ends. But like any other institution it is made for man, not man for it. Russians believe marriage should never become a prison house from which there is no escape when love is dead, nor a penal colony for mismated couples who cannot live happily together.

In sweeping away the old Czarist man-made laws which so often victimized women, and at times men, the revolutionaries doubtless often went too far and lost some elements of value. The first tentative marriage laws were codified in July, 1918. In the nine years that followed it was found that at many points the code needed revision. Before the law was revised it was characteristically submitted to nation-wide mass discussion. Women's organizations, as especially concerned, took the lead. Newspapers, magazines, men's clubs and youth organizations discussed every phase of the law for months. They were uncontrolled by the dead hand of the past, by propriety, precedent or technical legality. The one question was, what was rationally and experimentally best for all concerned, especially for children, for women, for men, for the home, for the nation? Stimulated by a flood of printed matter, over six thousand public meetings were reported in the villages alone, with countless debates, discussions and lectures. The whole national life at this point was in the crucible to be poured into fresh molds. Finally on January 1, 1927, the new revised marriage law was adopted. It will be amended further in the future as experience may dictate.

According to the present law, although a *de facto* marriage entails the same rights and duties as a registered marriage, civil marriage is recognized as legal, by registration at the registry office. A church marriage may follow if desired but is without legal significance. The conditions required for the registry of the marriage are mutual consent, the attainment of the matrimonial age of eighteen for both parties, with a signed statement that the marriage is entered into voluntarily, that there are no legal bars to the marriage, and that the parties are mutually informed as to the state of each other's health. Persons found guilty of making false statements are liable to prosecution by law. The parties may retain their previous surnames or they may adopt the name of either the husband, as is usually done, or the wife. Property remains the separate possession of each. Although the sexes are recognized everywhere as equal the chief purpose of the law is to protect the child and the woman.

A marriage may be dissolved during the lifetime of the parties, either by mutual consent or at the desire of either of them. No grounds for divorce are required. If it is by mutual consent a document is registered stating the agreement with regard to the property involved or the children if there are any. If there is a disagreement on these points the matter is referred to a court of law. Marriage for sex gratification with immediate divorce is punishable by law. The marriage laws of Russia resemble somewhat the modern code of Norway, but no period of waiting before the granting of the divorce is required in Russia as in Scandinavian countries.

It might be supposed that laws of such freedom might produce an orgy of sex gratification and divorce. Such has not been the case. Divorce is slightly more prevalent in Russia than in America.[1] They do not however bemoan this fact nor try to enforce or perpetuate marriages devoid of love or happiness. Promiscuity is condemned and monogamy is the ideal. The Soviet Government has preserved the monogamous marriage as the fundamental social unit, believing that mothers are better fitted than the state or its institutions for the care of babies. As Lunacharsky

---

[1] During the first half of 1927 there were 526,692 marriages and 126,-280 divorces in European Russia. This would imply one divorce to every four marriages. In America the proportion is one to six. In the most advanced city of Moscow there were 12,825 marriages and 9,973 divorces during the same period, while in a few cities in the U. S. A. at certain periods there have been more divorces registered than marriages.

says: "The main kernel of society, which must be in the center of our attention, is the family." Nevertheless, while the home is the social unit, of utmost value, it is not conceived as the sacred, absolute entity that it is in the West. It has large relative value; but it is only the state or society as a whole that has absolute value. It must be remembered that, with rare exceptions, home life at its highest and best was little known in Czarist days. Most families were either too poor, or too rich, or too untrained for the fully shared, cultured, affectionate, common life of the home. The finest home life has hardly been lost for it was scarcely found in Russia save in a small middle class.

The life of the children is lived more in the nursery, the school and the youth organizations, and somewhat less in the home than in other countries; and that of both men and women more in the factory, on the farm, in the trade union, the Party, the social clubs and the parks, and somewhat less in the bare, unattractive or overcrowded living quarters provided by the still inadequate housing accommodations of the cities. Russia never nationalized its women or its children but its home life must be the creation or evolution of the unknown future.

Prostitution is regarded as a characteristic of capitalistic countries and the commercializing of vice is viewed with moral indignation. The writer has gone through sections of Moscow and Leningrad which were the licensed quarters in Czarist days, but which today are probably more free from this vice than any of the cities of Europe. The shelterless waifs and homeless children left in large numbers by the famine, when three millions perished, have also now been mostly accommodated in children's homes and farm colonies.

Both abortion and birth control are legal, but the former is regarded as a necessary evil for needy women in poverty or ill health, and Russia is not yet sure enough of herself in the event of possible military invasion drastically to limit her future by unlimited birth control. But information may be freely obtained by anyone seeking it and knowledge of contraceptive methods will probably spread rapidly.

Maurice Hindus writes: "The Russians are an unrepressed and an uninhibited people. They are not overburdened with sex consciousness. Sex is to them a vital but not an all-absorbing object in life. They do not play with sex. This sex-unconsciousness the revolutionaries are seeking to perpetuate. They are death on commercial exploitation of sex. They have closed the old houses of prostitution. The injection of sex lure in any form into commercial life they have likewise banned. There is nowhere a hint of sex in the displays in shop windows or in the amusement places. There is scarcely a trace of sex suggestiveness in Russian motion pictures. If a Russian producer were to make sex intrigue the central point of interest in a picture he would be mercilessly howled down. The Russian public would not be stirred. The Russian newspapers and magazines are singularly free from sex scandals or sex tales. . . . Yet despite the emotional earnestness of the Russian woman, the sex unconsciousness of the Russian people, the measures of self-discipline that are a part of the new education of Russian humanity, one cannot help wondering if the

Russians are in danger of sinking into a morass of animality.
. . . Of course if in the end it should prove that under the
Russian condition of liberty, libertinism will diminish and
men will become less given to promiscuity and women will
remain as disinclined toward promiscuity, or more so than
tradition holds them to be, we shall have a new form of
monogamy in the love-life of human beings, the highest yet
attained, if only because it will flow out of inner desire and
be free from outward compulsion." [1]

The Youth Movement.

The Youth Movement of Russia is a new and bold experiment.   An organized youth movement began some thirty
years ago in Germany.   But Russia has today unquestion-
ably the most remarkable youth movement of the world.
The Komsomal or Union of Communist Youth held its first
conference in 1918 when there were only 22,000 members.
Today there are 2,466,000 members.   If we add the junior
Pioneers and Octobrists with their 3,301,458, we have a
total of nearly six million in this virile and rapidly growing
movement.[2]   Its quality is more remarkable than its quantity.   These youth organizations became an educative organ
for training a whole new generation of Russia in the principles of its new social order.   Instead of inculcating an
exclusive patriotism for "my country right or wrong," now
for "the first time in history" they seek to train a new youth

---

[1] Maurice Hindus, *Humanity Uprooted*, pp. 96-100.
[2] Statistics from Gosplan Statistical Department, September 1930.

and to re-train a whole adult generation for the workers of the world and a new revolutionary society.

There is an overlapping in the ages of the various divisions of the youth organizations. The Young Octobrists include children from 8 to 11, the Pioneers 10 to 16, the Komsomals 14 to 23, while at 18 the fortunate one-quarter to a third of the members are found worthy to enter the coveted Party. Like the Party, each of these organizations has its strict periodic "cleansing" to prune away the fruitless branches. No movement asks so much of its youth, challenges them with such a call to sacrifice or meets such a response of enthusiastic service.

The Young Octobrists are organized in brigades of twenty-five, in five links of five each, with one Pioneer in each. The Pioneers are grouped in detachments of sixty, divided into six links of ten each, who are helped in their training by the older Komsomals. The whole system is organized for intensive training in the new citizenship.

The young Pioneer has his five laws and five customs. The Pioneer "does not smoke nor drink nor swear." There are no paternal prohibitions from elders. These things simply "are not done." He is trained to take his daily exercise, he aims at knowledge, he develops his social and political activities in the school. Above all "the Pioneers are faithful to the workers' cause and to the commandments of Lenin." [1] There are weekly excursions under a Komsomal

---

[1] The five logs at his camp fire always symbolize the five continents of one common humanity. His badge reads "For the struggle in the cause of the workers, be ready." For an excellent account of Russia's train-

leader to museums, farms and factories. A member of the youth movement is given responsibilities but almost no privileges. He is taught the importance of family ties and of building up the new family in cleanliness, sanitation, fresh air and literacy, and to place the picture of Lenin and the "red corner" in every home. The old wife-beating or child-beating is no longer to be allowed and the Pioneer is to combat "the prejudice of religion." All his games are to develop collective and cooperative action and aims. From the first he is taught that the great ambition in life is not to seek success for one's self, but liberation and development of abundant life for all the workers of the world, without regard to race. The writer witnessed a meeting of some fifty thousand Pioneers in a great stadium in Moscow gathered from all over the world. There was a negro boy from Harlem, and boys from the slums of New York and Philadelphia. When over the loud speaker, the orator of the moment, warning of a capitalist invasion of Russia or a drive upon the workers in other lands would ask, "Pioneers, are you ready?"—the shout of the fifty thousand in unison, like a college cheer, was always, "We are ready."

These Pioneers, ten to sixteen years of age, own their own press and publish their own literature. The older Komsomals publish sixty newspapers and twenty magazines. Their paper *Young Communist Truth* is probably the best edited and most influential youth paper in the world, with a circulation of several hundred thousand over the whole U. S.

ing in citizenship see *Civic Training in Soviet Russia,* by Prof. Samuel Harper of the University of Chicago.

S. R. A stern self-discipline under their own codes charac-
terizes the whole movement. As the writer compares this
new youth of Russia with that before the war it seems like
another country. There is a new psychology produced by
this new environment and new system. There is a new
aggressive initiative in place of the former dreamy Russian
and the casual Slav. There is a new enthusiasm for athletics, for organization, for constant parades and demon-
strations, for earnest speech making. There is a new dignity
of labor, an enthusiasm for sacrifice, a militant drive and
mobilization on all "fronts" for the workers' cause, a new
discipline and self-government, a new precocity and ma-
turity, a new dynamic socialization of youth. The movement at its best is not a negative "revolt" against elders but
a positive and creative crusade for a great human objective.
While the Japanese government and police seek to suppress
"dangerous thoughts" of their radical students, these Russian youth have a drive of their own against all "dangerous
thinking" of reformist, capitalist or compromising tendencies.

The mature and responsible social service undertaken by
these militant youth is difficult for other countries to understand. During the recent harvests when thousands of the
miners returned to their rural fields and bolted to their
homes, instantly on call many thousands of Komsomals were
ready to step into their places in the mines that there might
be no halt in the five year program's strategic output of coal.
When some official had blundered and the peasants' potato
crop was called in all at once to Moscow, and they were in

danger of losing it within two weeks of the freezing of the Russian winter, instantly the Komsomals leaped into the breach and in a fortnight had the whole crop safely stored. When again there was an epidemic of automobile and other accidents, the Komsomals manned the street corners in a "safety first" campaign while new traffic habits were inculcated and the danger averted. Now comes the new law for "compulsory education" in Russia proper when the Government has not the buildings, equipment nor other provisions to make the law effective. Humanly it is impossible, but these organized youths are ready to tackle just such impossibilities and now a drive is on, headed by these practical youngsters, to make the law not a dead letter but a living reality. Under the Anti-alcoholic Society the youths march on a factory and demand of their parents that they sign a pledge to stop drinking. They meet the workers at the closing time of the factory with their posters and banners and temperance slogans and carry their crusade to the adult population. In a score of social, political and moral movements they are a growing force in the nation's life.

When one contrasts the youth of certain other lands, with their jazz, their "petting parties," their automobiles, their "get rich quick" ambitions, their measurement of values in terms of personal possession and competitive individual acquisition, one wonders, not whether there is anything to learn in this great laboratory of life, but whether we shall be willing to learn it and learn it in time. In the meantime the foreign press chiefly pictures the demoralization of youth in a supposed sexual orgy, and two social orders, each having so much to learn, are living in two worlds apart.

Here is a close-knit, sternly disciplined, aggressively articulate youth movement that is a powerful training ground for citizenship in the new order. Space permits but a single illustration to show concretely how Russian youth is trained in service. We shall take the case of Ellen, a girl of twenty. After she had been prepared and disciplined in the movement, she was assigned to the task of training younger Pioneers in the city and summer camps. Instead of repressive rules imposed from above she sought rather to incorporate principles in a program of action. There were excursions, parades, discussion groups and a weekly council. There was training in citizenship and in character building. All must be taught the history of the youth movement, of the Party and of the Revolution in the world movement. There were groups for dramatics, art, poetry, original writing and public speaking, and in the laws and customs of the Pioneers mentioned above.

After this work with Pioneers, Ellen was assigned responsibility for the development of a backward village. She found it illiterate, superstitious, sodden. The youth, in revolt against their elders, were drinking, gambling, dissipated and ignorant. With the cooperation of the authorities in Moscow this village must be changed. She gave every Sunday and two nights a week to voluntary service in this village. First of all she had to make sure that the village had a good school and a capable teacher. Soon she helped them democratically to secure a social center, with a library, reading room, radio, recreation room and a place for the meeting of groups. Next she organized the youth and encouraged them to lead a drive against drink, gambling, swearing and sexual dissipation. She brought out the powerful anti-drink film and a weekly moving picture with a social message, and some of the best lecturers from the city. In place of the icy roads for the young people's sleds which were a nuisance and a danger to the older women, she persuaded the young people to throw ashes on the roads, and then led the whole village to turn out and build a proper slide for winter sports. Soon all were sliding, old and young. After a year of such service there were marked signs of change in the life of the village, especially through its youth movement.

For her next task Ellen was assigned by her Komsomal council to the organization of sixteen neighboring villages, sending out the youth workers and training them to do in these other villages just what she had done in hers. After this she became one of the editors of the paper, *Young Communist Truth*. Then she was made manager of the press bureau of the district where she was in touch with all the editors of these papers, seeking to develop a concerted policy on behalf of youth. All of this service, was, of course, voluntary, unpaid and democratic, and all was carried on by the youth themselves.

When the writer last saw this girl she was a student in the university. She was occupied in service eight hours a day outside of her scholastic work. She was working not only among the students of Russia but by correspondence in five languages with the students of other European countries. Undoubtedly this service will interfere with her scholastic work. But she is gaining practical education in the vast complex of real life. One's mind travels far in other countries to recall a girl or boy, a member of a student movement or of an endeavor society, thus pouring out life in such joyous and effective service, training youth, transforming villages, writing, speaking, organizing, serving. Here is a vast laboratory of life with youth in its molten crucible. Is it possible that they have nothing to learn from the older nations? Is it possible that the western world has nothing to learn from a new kind of "flaming youth" which says: "Always remember that for us the world is just beginning"? Is it possible that both sides have nothing better to do than to prepare for a possible warfare of destruction or to be poisoned by false propaganda on both sides, which represents, and often misrepresents to each other, only the worst in these two systems?

CHAPTER VIII

LAW AND JUSTICE

As in almost every other department of life the entire legal structure of Czarist Russia has been swept away and new conceptions and codes of law have been substituted. Civil and criminal law have been codified.[1] The system of courts includes the People's Court, the Provincial Courts and the Supreme Court, as well as a number of special tribunals. In the People's Court all the judges are workingmen and nine-tenths of them belong to the Communist Party. The judge sits with two assessors and the case is decided by a majority vote. The court is more informal than in other countries, with little concern for legal technicalities and verbal hairsplitting, but with a primary concern for equity and essential justice.

Legal codes and procedure are affected by the new conception of class justice. No profession is made of settling disputes upon a basis of absolute or of abstract justice. If the offender is a poor worker he is given a light sentence; if he is an intelligent or privileged citizen who should have known better, or who has exploited his weaker brother, he is given a heavier punishment; but if he is a member of the Communist Party he is given the maximum penalty of the

---

[1] The Civil, Criminal, Land and Labor Codes have been followed by special Commercial, Family and other codifications.

145

law. Everything in Russia is conditioned by the fundamental dictatorship of the proletariat, by the conception of the state as the instrument of class domination; where liberty will be a reality only when economic class conflict has been abolished. In the meantime they endeavor to provide justice for the nine-tenths of the population that now make up the laboring and peasant classes.[1]

Both society and law are socialized in Russia. Penalty is measured not so much by personal guilt as by the social consequences of an act. Far worse than individual murder which takes the life of a single person, for which the ordinary penalty is from eight to ten years in prison, is a crime against society, or the state, which may wrong a multitude. Crimes punishable by death include counter-revolution, malfeasance in public office, and exploiting the superstitions of the masses for the overthrow of the state, etc.

Another distinguishing feature of the Soviet legal system is based on its different conception of property. With land

---

[1] Lenin in his *State and Revolution* writes: "The dictatorship of the proletariat—that is, the organization of the advance guard of the oppressed as a ruling class for the purpose of crushing the oppressors—cannot produce merely an expansion of democracy. Together with an immense expansion of democracy—for the first time becoming democracy for the poor, democracy for the people, and not democracy for the rich—the dictatorship of the proletariat will produce a series of restrictions of liberty in the case of the oppressors, exploiters and capitalists." Krylenko in his *Court Structure of the R. S. F. S. R.* writes: "For us, for the workers' and peasants' state, no form of court is acceptable except one which always and under all conditions will guarantee the defence of the interests of the workers. All state authority is nothing but a weapon of social force and constraint, with the aid of which a given governing class in a given society realizes its political sovereignty and guards its economic sovereignty."

and practically all means of production in the hands of the state the sphere of ownership has been greatly curtailed; much greater security has been given to life, and opportunity for the exploitation of others has been reduced. A man may have his home, his garden, his clothes and effects for his own use. He may have personal possessions for use but not functional property for power or exploitation of others by profit, interest or rent. If, so long as he usefully functions in society, he is provided for from birth to death, through unemployment, illness, accident and every contingency, what reason or excuse is there for the hoarding of fear or selfish acquisitiveness? The wealth that one may privately possess or leave to others is restricted by steeply graded taxes. Any amount of property may be willed, but in excess of $5,000 inheritance taxes reach 90 per cent.

A further characteristic of the whole penal system, insofar as it applies to the nine-tenths of the population who are workers, is that it is not vindictive or expiatory but redemptive. One must always make the regrettable exception of their treatment of their class enemies which is often cruelly unjust. But apart from them and the secret police, their penal system is probably the most modern, the most humane, the most redemptive in the world. The man whom a capitalistic society brands as a criminal they count a little brother who has gone wrong, perhaps through no fault of his own, because of poverty, ignorance, neglect or social injustice. He is never called a criminal nor put in a "prison." He wears no prison garb, no brand of Cain. He is paid the wages of a worker; he is allowed to talk, to smoke, to do any reasonable thing during the time of his sentence, which is often indeterminate. The effort is to redeem him from himself and to make him a useful citizen in society.

In a Rehabilitation Colony of the G. P. U. the boys are placed under their own self-government where it is the aim to teach them a trade and the joy of work. There are no armed guards or keepers. The elders are their friends and advisers, but the boys are their own rulers. The director is the only representative of the police in the institution, and he is a father and a friend rather than an official. There are no walls, no fences, no guards. The inmates are allowed to seek recruits in the regular prisons and take out promising youth who wish to embrace the opportunity for self discipline by entering a Rehabilitation Colony. Thieves and pickpockets are taught a trade and the cause of their crime thereby removed. They are provided with creative work, entertainment and athletic equipment in a character-building environment. The Colony near Moscow, which anyone may inspect, was begun a few years ago by a physician and a group of boys whom he sought to reclaim. There are now 1132 boys and men, and some women in the Colony. Those on good behavior may go home on vacation in the summer. They may marry while in the Colony; they may do almost anything that will serve to make them useful citizens. The Colony is forming the nucleus of a surrounding settlement or city which is being built up of men who were once criminals, but who may remain here for life if they wish to do so, as many of them do. They choose their permanent life work in the surrounding farms and factories which are built to accommodate them.

Members of this Rehabilitation Colony are carefully chosen from other penal institutions. Upon entering the grounds their past is forgotten. No questions are asked since it is assumed that each member will be a good citizen. Faith is a factor in reclamation. For a short time the newcomer is watched and guided. As he becomes adjusted, this supervision is relaxed, and ended as soon as possible. Full freedom to leave the Colony is granted, but few wish to go. The whole plan is humane, scientific and experimental in method. Each boy or girl is given some congenial work to do. Boys are not asked to make automobile license tags or ladies' shoes, but skates, athletic goods or articles in which they are interested. Girls are interested in clothing and often work the looms. They enjoy the same working hours, wages and protection as the trade unions offer. They love the colony like the boy who presented John Dewey with a painting on the back of which he had written that it was given in memory of "the school that opened my eyes." How many of the inmates of Sing Sing, of Auburn, of the long notorious San Quentin would choose to remain near the scene and under the influence of the beloved colony that opened their eyes? How strange that under this dictatorship, yes, under the very "terror" of the G. P. U., there should exist such a redemptive penal system, while in the free democracy of the land of Thomas Mott Osborne the prison system should so often be obsolete, inhuman, penal and vindictive.[1]

It gives an American a rude shock to come from a great redemptive Reclamation Colony in Russia to see the American motion picture, "The Big House," which pictures the penal system existing in the United States to crowded audiences in Europe. If American prisons are half as bad as this film portrays them they are a disgrace to any civilized country in the twentieth century. Instead of being redemptive the system appears to be vindictive, inhuman, a factory of crime, a maker of criminals. So long as the American prison system is in such crying need of reform her citizens cannot justly hold other countries in contempt or believe that there are no lessons to be learned from them.

Just as Disraeli spoke of two nations in other countries, the rich and poor, there are also two classes in Russia, the once poor nine-tenths, and the once rich or privileged one-tenth. The pyramid of privilege in Russia has been turned upside down. In the process the apex has been crushed. It would sometimes seem that they have almost sought to make Russia a heaven for the poor and a hell for the rich. In some measure they have succeeded. On the one hand there is class justice and many advantages for the workers. They have manifold privileges which they never knew under Czarism. Speaking of them after a study of civil liberties in Russia, Roger Baldwin writes: "The Russian people

---

[1] We shall speak in another connection of the treatment of the unfortunate one-tenth, of political and religious prisoners, and of all suspected of being class enemies.

enjoy more essential liberties than at any time in their history, and more of some sorts than any people in the world."[1] Concerning economic liberties he points out that the whole land has been freed from the domination of privileged classes living by the exploitation of labor. The peasants now have the land, instead of the landlords, and they govern their villages with little or no outside interference. The encouragement of cooperatives, machine farming, improved agriculture, the protection of the poor against rich exploiters, a steadily enriched social life in education, recreation in villages that for centuries were static and semi-barbarous, have not been unrecognized even if the forcible transition from competition to cooperation has been somewhat painful. The release of new creative energies among great masses of peasants and workers has been as remarkable as it has often been unconscious to themselves. Complain as they always have and probably always will, multitudes of them would fight to the death against any who tried to wrest from them their possessions and restore the Czarist system of landlords and employers.

The industrial workers have a larger participation in controlling their wages, their working conditions and even the political state than in almost any other country. A universal eight-hour day has been reduced to nearly seven, and a six-day working week to four. The worker cannot be arbitrarily dismissed without the consent of the trade union. Education and medical attention are free to all workers. Even politi-

---

[1] *Liberty Under the Soviets*, p. 5.

cally the Constitution guarantees that: "All authority is vested in the entire working population of the country."

While the Russians number almost two-thirds of the population, the nearly sixty millions in the national minorities are protected in their civil liberties and in their more than one hundred languages and autonomous educational systems. This is in striking contrast to the crushing of such minorities in Czarist Russia or Fascist Italy and is hardly equalled elsewhere in the world. All race prejudice or racial discrimination of any sort is fought both by law and by propaganda. One acute observer remarks: "Freedom from race prejudice is probably greater in Russia than in any country of mixed population in the world."

On the other hand, under a confessed dictatorship, however "temporary" it may hope to be, civil liberties are abridged as in few countries in the world. There is a universal censorship of all means of communication, and the complete suppression of any organized opposition. As understood in Anglo-Saxon countries there is no liberty for opponents of the régime. There is no organized freedom of speech or assemblage, nor of the press. No political liberty is permitted. Legality is confined to one Party, and within that, opposition, whether from the right or the left, against majority decisions or the group in power is dangerous. The numbers now in exile, never permitted to be known, of political or religious prisoners, sufficiently attest this denial of liberty.

Under a burning crusade the masses might not only tolerate but welcome the "divine right" of a prophet in

Arabia or a proletariat in Russia. But in a highly cultured community it would be intolerable to have a relatively small Party, or section of it, controlling all news and editorials. There is no privately owned free press in Russia. Every newspaper is issued either by some committee of the Communist Party, by a Soviet, or trade union, or public organization whose policies are controlled by orthodox Communists. The Russian worker, economically relatively free, would not exchange his solid rights for the privilege of casting his ballot under an abstract system of political liberty controlled by a possessing class. But neither would the cultural citizen of a free country surrender his right of habeas corpus, and willingly be liable to arrest upon suspicion of a political or economic offense, held in confinement, secretly tried without counsel or witness, and exiled, unknown, under a dreaded political police. Each system is looked upon with horror by members of the other. The former palaces and resorts of the rich now inhabited by happy workers on their vacations may be visited by all, but not so the dreaded Solovyetzky Island in the cold White Sea of the north, inhabited by political and religious prisoners. Russians should be as ashamed of such places as should Americans of their unreformed prison system, the indefinite confinement of men like Mooney and Billings, or the gang war of misgoverned cities like Chicago.

The Communist Party was intended to be democratic in the form of its organization; and it may yet become so, but the expulsion of its opposition, the only openly critical political force left in Russia, dangerously narrows its democracy to what might easily become an insufferable tyranny, were it not for its hardy working class and newly released rugged peasantry which are its hope and bulwark.[1]

The soviet system promises ultimate liberty and democracy, but it is deferred to that miraculous millennium of the future in which the credulous communist is asked to believe. As a compensation for the forfeiture of present liberties it requires as much faith as belief in a future heaven in lieu of justice here on earth. Both systems must be judged not by future promises but by present realities. Capitalism gives a measure of present liberty and promises future justice; communism seeks to give immediate social justice for the poor and promises future liberty.

Lenin maintained in May, 1917 that the constitution of the democratic republic of Russia must insure: "1. The sovereignty of the people. . . . 2. Universal, equal, and direct suffrage for all male and female citizens, twenty years old or over. . . . 3. The secret ballot at elections. . . . 4. Inviolability of person and dwelling. 5. Unlimited freedom of religion, speech, press, assembly, strikes and unions. 6. Freedom of movement and occupation, etc." [2]

Yet he writes in his *State and Revolution*: "Only in Communist Society, when the resistance of the capitalists has finally been broken, when the capitalists have disap-

---

[1] Bukharin writes: "When the proletariat is in power it cannot permit the enemies of its class to become judges . . . The judges are elected by the workers alone. The judges are elected solely from among the workers. For the exploiters the only right that remains is the right of being judged." *A B C of Communism*, p. 229.

[2] Lenin, *Collected Works*, Vol. I, p. 337.

peared, when there are no longer any classes, only then does the State disappear, and can one speak of freedom. Only then will be possible, and will be realized, a really full democracy, a democracy without any exceptions. And only then will democracy itself begin to wither away by virtue of the simple fact that, freed from capitalist slavery . . . people will gradually become accustomed to the observance of the elementary rules of social life, known for centuries, repeated for thousands of years in all sermons. They will become accustomed to their observance without force, without constraint, without subjection, without the special apparatus of compulsion which is called the State."

Bukharin writes: "Why, indeed, do we need the dictatorship: We need it for the *organized* destruction of the bourgeois régime; we need it that we may crush the enemies of the proletariat *by force*. Quite openly we say, by force. The dictatorship is the axe in the hands of the proletariat. Anyone who is opposed to the dictatorship of the proletariat is one who is afraid of decisive action, is afraid of hurting the bourgeoisie, is no revolutionist. When we have completely vanquished the bourgeoisie, the need for the dictatorship of the proletariat will no longer exist. But as long as the life-and-death struggle continues it is absolutely incumbent upon the working class to crush its enemies utterly. An epoch of proletarian dictatorship must inevitably intervene between a capitalist and a communist society." [1]

---

[1] *A B C of Communism*, p. 82.

CHAPTER IX

With the conversion of Vladimir of Kiev in 988 A. D., Russia began to adopt the Greek form of worship with the Byzantine imperial tradition from Constantinople, the second Rome, as Moscow in time became a third Rome. Peter the Great in 1721 abolished the patriarchate and became, with all succeeding Czars, the head of both church and state. The church became not only the chief support of the autocratic state but its subservient tool and, with the police, the most reactionary weapon of Czarist despotism. The confessional was often an agency of espionage and the priest the policeman of the Czar. Along with much genuine piety of peasants and the poorer clergy, the hierarchy was often rich, powerful and corrupt and almost everywhere stood for reaction. The life in many monasteries was a scandal, and the bogus, miracle-working mummies of the "incorruptible" bodies of the saints were a symptom of the official degradation of the church. Its crowning shame, however, was in the drunken and sensuous Rasputin, the "holy devil" who gained such power over the superstitious Czar Nicholas and his consort and wielded such malign influence over some of the higher officials. Against such a caricature of religion, which was all they had ever known, the persecuted revolutionary leaders in prison, exile, or banishment, determined to destroy both church and state in the name of a common humanity which they believed had for centuries suffered under both. After the revolution the Patriarch declared open war on the new republic and worked for the restoration of the Czarist régime.[1] This whole background must be remembered if we are to understand the present attitude of the authorities in Russia toward the church. This is the religion that they regard as an opiate or poison.

The type of religion developed in Russia was an esthetic mysticism.[2] Its services were the most beautiful, harmonious and reverent in the world. It was lacking, however, in moral fiber and in social vision. It was pietistic, otherworldly, individualistic and prevailingly anti-social. It stood for charity not social justice, for reaction rather than reform. Opinion is divided as to whether the peasant in old Russia was deeply mystical and religious or a "pagan beast."

---

[1] In the Patriarch's first message to the Church on January 19, 1918, he thus censures the excesses of the revolution: "That which you do is not only a cruel deed: it is verily a Satanic deed, for which you are condemned to hell fire . . . We conjure all you faithful children of the Orthodox Church not to enter into any kind of association with these monsters of the human race." Archbishop Evdokim admits: "It is not surprising that the Government is suspicious of the Church. During the civil war the heads of the Church worked in open sympathy with the enemies of the republic."

[2] "The religious characteristics of the Russian soul are: restless yearning and searching for God and divine truth, love of suffering and the sufferer, admiration and sympathy for social outcasts, the spirit of forgiveness, resignation and non-resistance to wrong, and finally, devotion to sacred symbolism and aesthetic mysticism. Thus religion in Russia is, first and foremost, worship and meditation. . . . The Russian National Church never was a preaching and a teaching church. It was, and is today, an institution of worship." *Religion Under the Soviets,* J. H. Hecker, p. 8.

Probably he was both. As in no other land coachmen, peasants and people crossed themselves before every ikon, shrine, or church with the prayer, "Lord be merciful." But it is also true today that many peasants have chopped down the wayside crosses for firewood, smoked up their Bibles for cigarette paper, and profess to be atheists today, as once they professed orthodoxy. Indeed, it is only a new, externally imposed, propagandized orthodoxy which they profess. Only when they are free shall we know what is in that sphinx-like, darkened peasant heart.

It is of the utmost importance that we understand the situation in Russia as a whole and especially the attitude of the Communist Party with regard to religion. Here are two great social orders, the capitalistic and the communistic, in conflict. The conflict is economic, political, social and religious. At no point do the systems come into more stark antagonism than upon the subject of religion, and at no point is it more difficult for them to understand each other. Understanding is difficult even where there is desire for it, but when both sides begin with an attitude of open hostility, and either credulously believe or eagerly welcome exaggeration, misrepresentation and false propaganda, it becomes almost impossible of achievement. We may remember also that intervention has been undertaken and wars have been fought for causes and occasions that were less. However much we may differ in opinion at this point, let us at least strive to understand.

The soviet leaders who had suffered under this system turned bitterly against the only religion they had known.

As the state church had enjoyed a practical monopoly of religious freedom and had encouraged the persecution of all other creeds, and pogroms against the Jews, in place of this state church the soviets established an anti-church state. From the time of Marx and Lenin they set their faces against religion conceived as an ally of superstition, an anti-social reactionary force and an other-worldly drug or soporific which refused social justice in this world while it promised compensation in the next.

We would do well to remember their suffering at the hands of religion in the past. But communists should also remember the historical past that makes liberal Americans particularly sensitive to religious persecution. The northern American colonies were founded by the Pilgrim Fathers in their endeavor to escape from the political and religious tyranny of the old world, just as Lenin and his comrades were endeavoring to escape from the worse tyranny of Czarism.

We would agree with communists in their condemnation of superstition and magic, in their acceptance of modern science, with all its implications and applications, including evolution, and in their determination to free the enslaved and superstitious masses. We would have great sympathy for a reverent agnosticism like that of Darwin's, but we would find bigoted, blatant and persecuting theism or atheism quite intolerable. And that quite apart from our personal beliefs. Not only scientists who believe in religion, like Millikan or Eddington, but men who do not share their beliefs, from Voltaire or Thomas Jefferson to Bernard

Shaw, all would be equally against a system which denied liberty of conscience and practice suffered for and won in part since the death of Socrates in 399 B. C. Thus the *Socialist Messenger* of the Russian Social Democratic Party, after stating that the majority of their members are non-religious, says: "But exactly for this reason we consider it our duty to raise our voice in loudest and most decisive protest against the persecutions which the church of all religions is suffering at present in Soviet Russia." [1]

Anglo-Saxons who inherit a tradition of tolerance and liberty, wonder why communists should desire to persecute religion. If it is a harmless superstition why not let it simply die out, by letting in the light of modern science and allowing the darkness to take care of itself. It is difficult to conceive how they can regard religion with such implacable hatred. In an effort to understand their position the writer has endeavored to draw up a comparison of where Christianity and Communism are in general agreement as to their humanitarian aims and where they are in inevitable contradiction and conflict in their beliefs, their methods and their ends.

In an effort to understand the attitude of the Government toward religion the writer obtained an interview with the highest Soviet official concerned in the matter. In view of the importance of his official statement we shall quote him almost in full. He said:

"You ask what is the present status of the Church and the policy of the Government toward religion. In the class war the clergy supported the White Guards and the monas-

[1] *Socialist Messenger*, Berlin, March 15, 1930.

COMMUNISM AND CHRISTIANITY

Comparison of Common Aims

1. Each seeks a new Social Order based on social justice and cooperation, in a classless society or equal brotherhood.

2. Each believes in a world-wide, universal missionary propaganda, personal obedience to the call for world service at any point of human need. Each seeks to capture and train youth, to make converts, to educate the illiterate. Each professes faith in the common man.

3. Each has unshaken faith in its mission, message and destiny. Each believes itself to be the hope of the world, the savior of humanity.

4. Each is an absolute system, claiming to be *the* way, expecting to conquer the world, and in large measure intolerant of all other ways and compromises. Each looks with aversion and condemnation upon the other.

5. Each believes in social service, personal sacrifice, absolute loyalty of the individual to the cause. Each in theory stands for the simple life, communal sharing, the condemnation of selfish accumulation and of unshared riches, generous giving, loyal support, care for the weak, responsibility for the poor, passion for social justice, moral indignation against social wrong and profiteering.

6. Each professes belief in a predestined rule of righteousness on earth where no government of force will be necessary.

7. Each has been persecuted and violently opposed; each believes in costly struggle. The orthodox section of each believes in an apocalyptic, cataclysmic, destructive world conflict, or Armageddon, before the new order can triumph—the one supernatural, the other natural, by the organized effort of the workers.

CONTRASTS

Communism	*Christianity*
1. A conception of the universe as materialistic mechanism of matter and blind force, the universe without a God, man without a soul, the individual without an enduring personality of absolute worth.[1]	The universe as the expression of intelligence and purpose of God as Father, Jesus as Elder Brother revealing the nature of the universe, man as a child of God of infinite worth.
2. Absolute loyalty to a cause, to the Revolution, to social control.	Absolute loyalty to individual conscience and to God.
3. Worldwide internationalism for one class, temporarily, their goal a classless society.	Worldwide internationalism for all humanity.
4. The motivation of class hate in the class war.	The authorized motivation of love alone.
5. An absolute dictatorship, as a means to an end.	Liberty of the individual—political, civil, religious.
6. Destructive revolution; government by coercion.	Constructive evolution; government by consent.
7. An immediate, new, creative, epoch of social justice by compulsion. Neglect of the individual for the sake of social salvation.	An ultimate reign of righteousness or social justice by moral suasion. But traditional alliance with the status quo, and long compromise with social injustice. Neglect of the social for the sake of individual salvation.

---

[1] There are two schools of philosophy in Russia, one of which is committed to atheism, the other may make room for a possible future theism.

teries were sometimes turned into fortresses against us.
The priests often led the people in counter-revolutionary
activity against the Government.   Many of the White Russians fled from the country after their defeat and have
abused and misrepresented us in France, America and
throughout the world.   When the Church was divided the
poorer clergy became more friendly to us, but the Reformed
or 'Regenerate' branch of the Church is only in the minority.
In the villages the religion of the churches is mostly magic
and superstition.   Our attitude was liberal in giving legal
status to religious bodies.   But counter-revolutionary forces
in the churches took advantage of our liberalism.   The
religious influence against us now is no longer monarchistic
but bourgeois, but it tends to ally itself with the Nepmen,
kulaks and intelligentsia, so that our enemies may form one
bloc against us.   They employ hired labor and are often
hostile to our economic program.   In our present socialization of agriculture we are in the midst of a life and death
struggle.   Any hostility to our economic program means to
us counter-revolution.   Any priest or minister who is against
our program of collective farming becomes thereby our political enemy.   Some use religion as a cloak to hide their economic
opposition.   The policy of the Government toward them is determined by their political and economic attitude and activity.

"Again, the religious bodies of Russia, especially among
the sects, have enormous foreign connections.   Money is sent
to them from abroad in subsidies.   These foreign organizations send in their religious publications and propaganda.
They even train ministers and religious workers abroad for

service in Russia. The foreign connections of the Baptists, Adventists and Evangelicals are characteristic of others.

"You ask regarding the recent change in the wording of the law and the constitution in regard to religion.[1] There has been no change in our principle of liberty or conscience. No religion and no faith as such is persecuted but only their political intrigues or economic opposition wherever such exist. Under our policy the magical and superstitious elements of religion are passing away. Our higher officials however have to restrain the local resentment and indignation of the masses against the churches in some places.

"You ask if there are any elements in religion that are *necessarily* antagonistic to the present policy of the Soviet Government. My answer is, Yes, religion is inevitably and absolutely hostile to the Soviet Government. These two systems are in necessary conflict and antagonism. We stand absolutely against all exploitation, human slavery and social injustice. Religion traditionally, and in Russia habitually, has sanctioned oppression. You stand for class peace, we for class war. Your Christian principles blunt the edge of this class war. I repeat that no person is persecuted for his religious beliefs but only for his political, social or economic hostility to our program.

"We are particularly concerned about religion in our schools and colleges for training youth. Regarding religion as we do as gross superstition we are anxious to insure the

---

[1] Religious and anti-religious propaganda and preaching were formerly equally allowed but now only religious worship is permitted while anti-religious propaganda is encouraged.

triumph of pure science in our educational system and to remove from the mind of youth all vestiges of superstition and
of the anti-social attitude that always accompanies religion.

"We understand that in many of your own universities,
as in Tennessee, they forbid the study of Darwin and evolution. You still have many *a priori* superstitious notions
left in your universities where religion seems still to linger,
but they are not in ours. Every scientist must be an atheist.
You say that in America you have liberty to teach theism or
atheism, religion or anti-religion, and you ask why we do not
let the people choose for themselves and believe what they
will. We say, *People do not believe what they will but what
they are told. And we propose to tell them!*"

It is not generally recognized by the majority of either
side how fundamental, widespread and how practically inevitable this conflict between the two systems is under present
conditions. For instance, the majority of communists will
assure one that there is no religious persecution whatever
in Russia today. Most of them would honestly and indignantly deny its existence. If so they simply do not know
the facts. In Russia, more than in any other land, people
are living today in two widely separated worlds.

It is one of the strange anomalies of Russian life that
under a class dictatorship opposed by hostile nations there
exists a fear psychosis and a consequent suspicion of or
contempt for other classes, so that life is lived by individuals
or communities largely in separate, water-tight compartments. No Christian knows what goes on in the secret
councils of the Political Bureau or the Communist Party.

And few communists know what persecution the Christian community is suffering.

Let us examine the communist statement that no religious persecution exists in Russia today. It has been the privilege of the writer to work among students throughout America, Asia and in many countries in Europe during the past thirty-five years. Russia is the only civilized land of which he knows where no Christian Student Movement or religious student meeting of any kind whatever is permitted. It is the only country where even three or four Christian students cannot meet in secret or in public to discuss religion. To his knowledge some Christian students have been imprisoned or banished on account of their religious beliefs, some are in exile, some have been expelled from the universities, while more are silenced, living their lonely lives in secret. This is the only country the writer visits where he does not know of a single university student who can openly profess his religious faith and remain unmolested.

The Constitution of Soviet Russia guarantees liberty of conscience and liberty of worship. The letter of the law is fulfilled, and to some extent its spirit, by permitting the majority of the places of worship to function, in connection with Christianity and all other religions. The writer found most of the churches which he visited holding regular services unmolested, and fairly well attended. Thus the Government keeps the letter of the law. The moment, however, that a priest or minister is found to be prophetic or effective, if he can reach students or youth or labor, any of the dynamic classes, he must be silenced at once or sent into exile. He is dealt with by the tribunal of the secret police, so quietly that often even the man's neighbors do not know what has happened to him. Some have been removed, some exiled, some have had their churches or places of worship closed upon one technicality or another, some have been expelled from their institutions, or had their publications suppressed, but almost all vital preachers or active religious workers have been silenced.

In most other respects conditions on the whole are better today than in Czarist Russia. But the writer does not find even a tithe of the religious liberty enjoyed under the old tyrannical régime. In this very city of Moscow, where we are now writing, although forbidden by the police, we conducted religious meetings for students before the war, with an attendance of two hundred a night, crowded on the floor of two adjoining students' rooms. Today in Soviet Russia we would not dare, for their sakes, to meet even four or five students in public or in private to discuss the subject of religion.

Eighteen years ago here in Moscow we formed friendships with some of the students. When we visited here seven years ago we could see them individually though we could not meet with even a small group to tell them what was going on in other lands in the student movement. Three years ago they begged us not even to call upon them. Today we dare not even meet them. Most Russians of the old intellectual or religious classes are now afraid to have any contact whatever with foreigners for obvious reasons.

The attitude of the Soviet leaders to religion is clear, consistent and implacable. As the matter is important we shall quote them somewhat at length. Lenin thus clearly states the official attitude of communists to religion in the early revolutionary days: "The philosophy of Social Democracy is based on scientific socialism, i.e., on Marxism. As Marx and Engels frequently declared, the philosophic basis of Marxism is dialectical materialism—a materialism which is absolutely atheistic and strongly hostile to all religion. . . . 'Religion is the opium of the people,' said Marx, and this thought is the cornerstone of the whole Marxian philosophy in the question of religion. Marxism regards all religions and churches, all religious organizations, as organs of bourgeois reaction, serving to drug the minds of the working class and to perpetuate their exploitation."

Lenin then endorses Engel's opposition to a war on religion as stupid and as the best means of reviving it. He maintains that religion is a private matter so far as the state is concerned but not as it concerns each party member. He continues: "Marxism is materialism. . . . We must combat religion. . . . The fight must be directed toward eradicating the social roots of religion. . . . The roots of religion today are to be found in the social oppression of the masses, in their apparently complete helplessness in face of the blind forces of capitalism. . . . We are resolutely opposed to offending their religious convictions in the slightest degree." [1]

Again Lenin says: "Religion is one of the forms of spiritual oppression, lying everywhere on the masses of the people. The helplessness of the exploited classes in their

---

[1] *Selections from Lenin,* Vol. II, pp. 269-279, *Collected Works,* Russian XI, pp. 250-260.

struggle with the exploiters just as inevitably generates faith in a better life beyond the grave as the helplessness of the savage in his struggle with nature produces faith in gods, devils, miracles, and so forth. To him who works and is poor all his life religion teaches passivity and patience in earthly life, consoling him with the hope of a heavenly reward. To those who live on the labor of others religion teaches benevolence in earthly life, offering them a very cheap justification for all their exploiting existence and selling tickets to heavenly happiness at a reduced price. Religion is opium for the people." [1]

Stalin thus states his position on religion: "The Party cannot be neutral in regard to religion. Communists who hinder the broadest development of anti-religious propaganda have no place in the ranks of the Party." [2]

Bukharin sums up the whole controversy when he says: "Religion and communism are incompatible both theoretically and practically." "The Christian code runs: 'Whosoever shall smite thee on thy right cheek, turn to him the other also.' In most cases there is an irreconcilable conflict between the principles of communist tactics and the commandments of religion." [3]

Released themselves from Czarist oppression, the first legislation and constitutional guarantees of the Soviets regarding religion were somewhat generous. [4]

---

[1] *Thoughts of Lenin About Religion,* by E. Jaroslavsky, p. 10.

[2] Interview with the American Labour Delegation, Sept. 15, 1927.

[3] *A B C of Communism,* Bukharin, English Edition, pp. 256, 257.

[4] The legal position of religion in Russia was guaranteed by the 13th article of the Constitution of the U. S. S. R. and by the decree of the

The Constitution at first granted equal freedom for religious or anti-religious propaganda. Article 5 of the Constitution of the R. S. F. S. R. in its former redaction read as follows: "In order to provide the workers actual freedom of conscience the church is separated from the state and the school from the church, while freedom for religious and anti-religious propaganda is recognized for all citizens." Thriving under this measure of religious liberty there was a rapid growth among the sectarians who appealed strongly to peasants, workers and youth, especially among the Baptists and Evangelicals. Communists were alarmed when these bodies soon trebled their pre-war following and reported several million adherents attending their services. After 1928 a more active anti-religious policy became apparent. This was evident in the change of the wording of the Constitution from "freedom for religious and anti-religious propaganda is recognized for all citizens," to

Soviet of the People's Commissaries, January 13, 1918; also by additional and explanatory legislative measures. According to the letter of these legislative acts, religion enjoyed relative freedom; they forbade the issue of local laws limiting freedom of conscience; also such laws as would grant certain prerogatives for the adherence to a certain religion or for the denial of all religion. They forbade that adherence to religion should entail the loss of any juridical rights, declaring that religion is the private business of a citizen. They guaranteed freedom of religious propaganda; they did not forbid the religious education of children by the parents at home; and persons having attained 18 years of age had the right to receive it in special institutions. They declared the liberty of Church organizations, conferences, congresses, of the religious press and of divine service. The only thing demanded by the law was that religion should be eliminated from state and public life; that religion should be declared the private business of every citizen.

"freedom for religious confession and anti-religious propaganda is recognized for all citizens."[1]

Under existing law, not less than twenty persons who have reached the age of eighteen years may form a recognized religious society or church. This group must be registered. Each person may belong to only one local group and each society may have the right to the use of only one place of worship. Religious bodies are forbidden all educational, philanthropic, social or practical activities. They are not allowed to form cooperatives, agricultural or industrial associations. They are forbidden "special meetings for children, youths, and women for prayer purposes . . . literary, needlework . . . excursions and children's gatherings, to found libraries and reading rooms, to organize sanatoria and medical assistance." Their church property is nationalized. The teaching of religion in any public or private educational institution is forbidden, but theological courses may be organized by special permission for those over eighteen years of age.[2]

In the beginning the soviet authorities were hostile to the Orthodox Church and relatively lenient to the sects who like themselves had been persecuted under the Czarist regime. The growth and success of the sects has made them reverse this attitude. The majority of the Orthodox churches, both in the cities and in the villages, are still open

---

[1] Redaction adopted by the Congress of Soviets in May, 1929. *Izvestia,* May 22, 1929.

[2] Decree of the All-Russian Central Executive Committee, *Izvestia,* April 26, 1929. See *Soviet and Religion,* Carnegie Endowment Series, No. 261, June 19, 1930, p. 303.

and regularly conduct services as they have ever since the Revolution. But most of the sectarian places of worship have been closed, together with their clubs, collectives and groups for cooperative labor.

Upon his annual visits to Russia the writer has always attended the churches, both in the city and in the country. Upon a Saturday night he visited eight churches in Moscow. They were almost, though not quite, as well filled as before the war. Men, women and girls were present. The boys and younger men were conspicuously absent so far as the workers and peasants were concerned.

In 1921 the authorities requisitioned the treasures of the churches and sold them for famine relief. Some ecclesiastical authorities who resisted were shot, exiled or imprisoned. There was open warfare between the atheist government and the Orthodox Church. The former exposed the frauds of the church by simply opening the coffins of the "incorruptible saints," exposing the dry bones, wax figures or bogus paraphernalia which had been used to hoodwink the superstitious masses in their pilgrimages to the sacred shrines and monasteries. There were also frequent excesses by mobs against hypocritical or unpopular priests and monks. The Patriarch declared open war upon the revolutionary government. The leaders of the church, national or local, often made common cause with the early anti-revolutionary forces for the overthrow of the government, and later at times with the *kulaks* and those who opposed the government plan for collective agriculture.

Government officials, communists and members of the

anti-religious organizations have in turn done all that they could to cripple the church. They have welcomed and fostered every evidence of a division or internal ecclesiastical quarrel. They have endeavored to discredit representatives of the hierarchy in the eyes of the clergy and people, to hinder or render difficult communication between the central authorities and local churches, to cripple theological education, to hinder the religious education of children while furthering anti-religious education. They have placed legal restrictions and increasingly heavy and multiplying taxation upon priests and parishes which have effectively "liquidated" many of them.[1] They have arrested or exiled many of the ablest and most earnest and effective leaders, leaving chiefly the formal, and apparently harmless, priests to conduct Orthodox services. They have closed the religious press and prevented religious propaganda. They have abolished the monasteries and many of the most honored shrines. Under the Third Section of the G. P. U. they have organized within the church among its own ministers and laymen, by fear, by economic pressure, by the methods of the third degree, a network of informers and agents to discover and eliminate the most influential and effective representatives of the church.[2] With all the civilized world, communists look with loathing and indignation upon the old secret police of the Czars and disfranchise them and their families.

---

[1] Rent for a small room for the clergy is abnormally high. Local assessments of "voluntary" taxation, and taxes in "kind," though the clergy are deprived by law from engaging in agriculture, tend to make their position impossible.

[2] Within recent years at least 196 bishops have been arrested and exiled.

Yet their own Third Section of the G. P. U. carries on its equally odious and loathsome work. So far as this activity is concerned, can they expect any other attitude toward themselves than that of the whole world toward the Czarist order's despicable police?

When the clergy are unable to fulfill the heavy demands of taxation their property is confiscated or sold at auction. Children of the clergy are frequently deprived of rights because of their origin. They are often not accepted in the schools and of course not in the universities. The clergy are refused medical aid. Since January, 1930, they have been deprived of the use of the mails, telegraph and telephone, of letters, money orders or parcels. This means hardship and suffering for the exiled clergy, and places them outside the law. According to government statistics fifty per cent of the present ministers of religion are over fifty years of age and only five per cent below thirty.[1] As theological preparation is limited or crippled this would point toward their final hoped for "liquidation."

To those accustomed to civil liberties and religious toleration of western countries, religious persecution would seem unthinkable in the twentieth century, but to the communist, liberty, democracy and toleration are only "bourgeois prejudices." Thus characteristically *Izvestia,* the official organ of the Government, writes: "Religious tolerance is, of course, an element of liberalism, yet it is proclaimed in our constitution. This element of liberalism is

---

[1] Statistics published by the Department of Religions of the People's Commissariat of Internal Affairs.

included by the communist party in its political and cultural practice by no means by reason of its being in any way inclined toward peace with any sort of popery, certainly not because of any weakening in our hatred towards religion and our endeavor to destroy it. On the contrary, by our religious tolerance we simply conveniently limit the field of struggle and decline to use a worthless weapon. Our country is still full of a great number of various sorts of believers. To challenge them to a final, decisive battle, to proclaim them persecuted because of 'prohibition of faith' would mean that we become supporters of the priests, because by such means we would immediately cast a significant part of these masses into the arms of the priests." [1]

In the light of the above we can understand the present drive against religion in the field of education. Krupskaya, Madam Lenin, said: "It is necessary more and more to inject a materialistic spirit into education, to energetically work with organizations of children, to develop in them the spirit of comradeship, to extricate more deeply the very roots of religion." [2]

Lunacharsky, former Commissar of Education, warned religious teachers, whom he estimated at still 30 or 40 per cent of the teaching force, as follows: "The believing teacher in the soviet school is an awkward contradiction, and departments of popular education are bound to use every opportunity to replace such teachers with new ones, of antireligious sentiments." In his speech before the Fourteenth

[1] *Izvestia*, June 8, 1929.
[2] *The Way to the New School*, August 7, 1928.

All-Russian Congress of Soviets he said: "All our cultural institutions . . . must be considered by us as working on the front for the repulse of the religious danger. . . . I should like in the most sadistic manner to root out and tear out somehow this very weed from our fields and gardens." [1]

During a former visit to Russia, in an interview with Rudziatak, then head of the Russian railways and member of the Political Bureau, he spoke with keen disappointment of an American business man who had just been in Russia selling his goods, because this man had appeared to be friendly to them but had bitterly criticized their whole regime after he had departed. It suddenly occurred to us that these leaders might say the same of our whole party, for we were most certainly going to criticize them upon our return to our own country. Accordingly we had an interview with Trotzky's sister, Madam Kamaneva, then the head of the Cultural Relations Society, and inquired if we could meet the Soviet leaders for a friendly conference to tell them exactly what we thought of their system, what we were going to say and write about it, and frankly bring forward our every criticism or indictment of it, thus giving them an opportunity to reply and state their side of the case, which we were anxious to hear.

Accordingly the meeting was arranged. Our party of twenty-four Americans held a caucus to discuss what appeared to be, in our opinion, the chief evils or defects in their system. Four of our number were chosen to present

[1] *Izvestia*, May 17, 1929.

the four principal indictments. These were handed in writing in advance to the Soviet leaders, and four of their number were chosen to present their side of the case. The four principal evils singled out were: their dictatorship with its severe abridgment of liberty; their policy of world revolution by violence; their attitude toward religion; and their relationship to other nations which did not encourage cooperation, recognition, loans, concessions or trade.

For four hours we attacked them unsparingly upon these four vulnerable points, and listened to the speakers they had chosen to state their case and defend their policies. Never in any other country or upon any other occasion have we been so brutally frank, so merciless in our criticism. Our arguments were received and replied to in the finest spirit. Both sides spoke with healthy realism and frank objectivity. It was one of the most interesting and enlightening discussions we had ever known.

The writer, who spoke second, asked: If the avowed communist objective was world revolution, involving the overthrow of existing governments, why should we grant them recognition or loans or any other cooperation? The writer also seconded the criticism of the preceding speaker as to their denial of liberty. In that very city of Moscow, under the unspeakable Czarist regime, which we condemned with them, we had been able to give lectures and conduct meetings for students as we had all over Russia for believers or unbelievers, theists, atheists or agnostics. Why then were we not free to do so under the present regime? Why was this the only government on earth, laying claim to be civilized, which did not permit public meetings or lectures for students upon the subject of religion?

When the editor of *The Godless* rose to reply he stated that there was nothing in their constitution, which guaranteed liberty of conscience, to prevent our holding such meetings. Upon this statement we challenged him to a debate upon the following Sunday upon the subject of religion—Theism versus Atheism. He immediately accepted the challenge and we agreed upon the terms of the debate. There were to be four speakers, two Christians, the writer and a Russian friend, and two atheists; each speaker was to be allowed an hour, with questions following.

A large hall was secured in the city, a notice was put in the papers and within forty-eight hours every seat was sold and the proceeds given to an orphanage, according to the agreement. We had expected to meet an audience of atheists and probably go down to a forensic defeat, in the hope of getting the door of tolerance or religious liberty opened just a little further. To our surprise, about one-third of the audience were Christians who boldly heckled the communist speakers, as the atheists heckled the Russian Christian who spoke. Some two hundred written questions were handed up to be answered, such as: "Please explain to us the relation between lynching and Christianity. We do not lynch people over here, nor deny them justice because of their color or race, but we understand that you do lynch negroes in Christian America. What is the relation of that practice to your religion?"

The debate began on a Sunday afternoon. In five hours

the hall had to be cleared for the next engagement. It is a good thing it had, or we might have been kept much more than five hours. In any event, it seemed to the writer that the proverbial interest of the Russian in religion was so vital and deep that nothing could ever uproot it from his heart. It seemed that no tyranny could be maintained forever even over a long-suffering population, and that once real liberty were granted religion would reassert itself again and find expression, as it always has in history, along with every other elemental and fundamental capacity of the human spirit.

We were impressed by the fairness of the chairman, of one of the Russian speakers and of most of the audience. The reports in the papers next day were as intolerant and as unfair as they could well be. But without a single privately owned or free paper in all Russia, no reply was possible and no statement of the other side of the case. As the Russian official said to us : "People believe what they are told. And *we* propose to tell them."

The willingness to have the debate at all was to their credit and indicated a measure of tolerance at that time. That was in 1926. Today things have "tightened up," both politically against all opponents of the group now in power, and religiously in the more determined drive against the churches, especially the once successful sectarians. No such discussion with the leaders and no such debate would be permitted or be possible today. In the almost kaleido-scopic changes which are continually taking place in Russia anything may happen in the future. For some years there will probably be a trial of strength and the determined endeavor to uproot the last vestiges of religion from the rising generation and from the dynamic classes—students, organized youth, members of the red army, the trade unions, the collective farms, and the schools.

In the opinion of many competent observers communists will have to take their choice between an endless tyranny seeking to make standardized robots, which no really awakened, critical and self-governing people with any initiative will permanently tolerate, and a liberty that will witness, if history repeats itself, the reappearance of religion among the classes where it has been temporarily eliminated.

Their propagandized atheism, which is a kind of fanatical religion, however they may abhor the term, is no more necessarily permanent than was the esthetic mysticism of their former Byzantine religion. One of the most powerful preachers in Russia today—for the moment silenced because no really powerful preacher is given freedom—was once a convinced atheist. There were villages in Siberia for a time converted from their orthodox religion to atheism by propaganda, which were for a time swept again into the stream of a new and vital religious life by some dynamic modern preacher of the free churches. Tyranny is no test of truth, and no measure of faith. Russia will have to choose eventually between liberty and tyranny. A people under the subjection of slavery, serfdom or religious oppression will never lead the world. Once they are granted liberty, or take it for themselves, we shall see whether atheism or theism is native to the human heart, whether irreligion or religion is natural. By their fruits the two systems will be judged. As long as there are slums, child labor, neglected unemployment, lynching, bootlegging and lawlessness prevalent under a system of liberalism and religion, the verdict may not be a foregone conclusion, save in the dogmatic, *a priori* claim of convinced religionists. If that is the best that religion can do in these economic and social areas after nineteen centuries in the world, and after four centuries of Czarism, it will take more than credal claims to justify it.

If, on the other hand, the communist system dare not even give the other side a hearing, if it claims a monopoly of all propaganda and power, and can only maintain itself by continued force—what test of truth does it offer and what hope of winning educated men in a world that is still intellectually free? On the one hand what is wrong if, after nineteen centuries, Christianity has not been tried and found wanting, but has not even been fairly tried? And, on the other hand, what claim can communism make upon free men if it dare not let anything be tried, save at the dictation or by the manipulation of an infinitesimal group within a small party? A proverbial visitor from Mars would probably conclude that however incommensurable and however great their disparity, here were two major systems both experimental and both on trial.

Russia is now in the midst of a prolonged battle between the forces of religion and anti-religion. In many homes we saw the ikons supplanted by pictures of Lenin. In others the ikon is in one corner and the picture of Lenin in the other, sometimes signifying a divided allegiance, either between the husband and wife, or in the heart of the same person. The most aggressive drive against religion today is conducted by the Militant Godless Society whose purpose, according to its constitution, is "active, systematic and continuous struggle against religion in all its forms and appearances." When the writer visited their headquarters in Moscow he found an able and earnest staff of voluntary workers, mostly professors and students, and a small paid executive. Their honesty, zeal and enthusiasm were transparent. For them, this was evidently a burning crusade to overthrow the greatest evil they knew, as the opiate or poison of the people, and to establish the new millenium of communism. They frankly and proudly explained their methods of work by magazines, posters, lectures and every possible form of propaganda. They took particular satisfaction in telling how they successfully closed the churches. They would go two by two to every apartment in the neighborhood of a church and ask whether the inmates would prefer to have the building used for purposes of worship on Sunday, or have it turned into a useful club or neighborhood house continually open for all. When they had secured the signatures of the majority of the neighborhood, they would petition the authorities to have the building confiscated for secular purposes. Thus they claimed that already more than half the churches of Moscow had been closed. If so, it would still be true that the majority of the 50,000 churches of Russia are open, though only a minority of the former 400,000 priests are still functioning. The Godless Society, together with the Government, publishes anti-religious textbooks for peasants. The Society has had more than twenty anti-religious motion pictures prepared for its campaigns. It sends out its lectures, speakers and propagandists like any other voluntary missionary society.

It is active in the red army and higher educational institutions. After their agitation the Presidium of the local Soviet Government prohibited the ringing of church bells in Moscow, and the city is now strangely silent.[1] Church bells have been removed from a number of the churches and metal factories have been supplied for some time to come.

Special "anti-religious universities" have been founded in thirteen cities to prepare leaders for their atheistic missionary campaign. The Godless Society publishes a number of papers and magazines.[2] In addition to these, during 1929, 507 anti-religious publications were issued. In a recent debate as to the most successful methods for their campaign, alarm was professed that two million young men had gone into various religious bodies, while the Society, on the other hand, professed to have at that time over two and a half million Militant Godless members.[3] Probably both figures would have to be taken with a grain of salt. The growth in membership claimed by the Society to date is as follows:

	1927	1928	1929	1930
Militant Godless Membership	98,402	123,007	700,000	3,000,000

[1] *Izvestia,* January 6, 1930.
[2] *The Anti-religious Worker,* designed for agitators and leaders, reaches 20,000; their bi-weekly magazine has 80,000 readers; their principal weekly journal, *The Godless,* claims a circulation of 375,000.
[3] Leningrad *Krasnaya Gazeta,* April 19, 1930.

The Society's anti-religious five-year plan proposes to increase this number from three to five-fold. Their militant methods, however, frequently produce an unfavorable reaction. An over-zealous campaign in the homes of the teachers in the Romensky region on Christmas eve so "frightened all the children" and caused such resentment that the Society recognized its mistake. Here, however, is a permanent working organization to be reckoned with like any other missionary society.

Early in 1930 the whole campaign for the collectives and against the *kulaks* and the church went to such lengths and excesses, and the world protest against the persecution of religion was so widespread, that it was followed by Stalin's article of March 2, 1930, regarding the collective movement on "Heads turned with success" in which he ironically attacks those who introduce collectivization "by beginning with tearing down the church bells." Following this the Central Committee of the Communist Party on March 15, 1930, spoke of the "entirely unpermissible deviations from the Party line in the area of struggle against religious prejudices," while Party organizations were "to definitely discontinue the practice of closing churches by administrative measures, covering themselves by fictitious voluntary social demands of the population."

The forces on the side of this anti-religious campaign are seemingly overwhelming. They claim some three million connected with the Godless Society. There are about two million members and probationers of the Communist Party; all of whom must be atheists. The red army numbering over 560,000 is made a special field for the anti-religious campaign. The movement is strong among the nearly 12,000,000 in the trade unions. Nearly 6,000,000 in the youth organizations are being trained in this crusade. It is also being organized in the whole educational system with the avowed object of rooting religion out of the minds of the rising generation. Pressure may also be increasingly brought to bear upon the one-quarter of the population already in the collectives and communes. Behind this crusade is all the concentrated wealth and power and propaganda of a determined dictatorship.

On the other side is a church that was never prepared intellectually, morally or socially to meet such an ordeal. Yet some of the priests, persecuted, reviled, over-taxed in their often abject poverty, and almost broken as some of them are, write: "There is no power, physical or moral, which can destroy in our people the holy Christian religion, still less uproot from the heart of man the idea of God." The same spirit that was manifest under the persecutions of Nero or Diocletian is reappearing in Russia today. It is as yet too early to foretell the outcome, except on *a priori* grounds. Certainly the church never had to meet in the persecution of the Roman Empire, intermittent, spasmodic, brutal, or stupid as it often was, what it has to face in this relentless, implacable, ruthless persecution of cold intelligence. On the one hand it need not be exaggerated by wild and hectic reports, nor on the other hand are the nations hoodwinked by the mere letter of the law or Constitution. It is not words but deeds that count.

The world should not underrate the intelligence, the conviction or the clear and consistent policy of the soviet leaders of Russia in this crusade against religion.   Nor on the other hand, should these leaders imagine that the rest of the world is stupid.   *What is done in Russia cannot be hid.* The church in Czarist Russia could not be hid.   A body that could expel the great Count Leo Tolstoi and let him die an excommunicate, and allow a drunken brute, Rasputin, to dominate Czar and Czarina, and sometimes officers of the army and members of the cabinet, could not be hid. Neither can the conditions in the Solovyetzky Island, nor some of the sadist persecutions of the Third Section of the Department of Secret Operations of the G. P. U.

People of America little realize how widely the world is still concerned with **Sacco and Vanzetti, and** with Mooney and Billings.   Leaders in Russia who think that, true to their picture, the greed of a "capitalist" society thinks only of concessions and trade, do not yet realize that the world cares far more about these moral and human conditions, just as it did in the Czarist regime.   We can only hope that the time will come when these evils will be corrected, and that we can commend them for a whole policy brought out into the open light of day, as we can now admire many aspects of their titanic five year plan and their magnificent economic progress in the face of terrific hardships and almost insurmountable obstacles.

CHAPTER X

We have asked ourselves, what is communism in theory and in fact, and how is it working in the U. S. S. R.? We have endeavored briefly to survey Russia's agricultural, industrial, and political life, its education and culture, its administration of law and justice, its attitudes and practices concerning moral and religious questions. Let us now seek, as impartially as we can, to evaluate the entire system. What are its defects and its possible values, and what influence is it likely to have for good or evil upon the life of the world?

Since the psychology of an opposing social order demands criticism first, what are the outstanding evils of the system? From our point of view there are essentially three: a dictatorship with its constant danger of tyranny, the policy of world revolution by violence and destruction, and an attitude of bigotry and intolerance which manifests itself in such matters as the persecution of religion. Let us consider each of these in turn.

1. *Dictatorship*

This dictatorship, though in aim democratic for the working class, sometimes takes the form of tyranny and sometimes of terror. In the age-long quest to solve the problem of the relation of the individual to society, the rights of the one and of the many, the question of freedom on the one hand and order on the other, the political pendulum tends to swing to the two extremes of anarchy and tyranny. As between an extreme individualism and a rigid collectivism, although conscious of the danger of both, communists have chosen the latter, and the western world of liberalism the former. At this point they are in striking contrast and in open conflict. Liberalism demands a maximum of personal liberty, communism an absolute social control.

Marx maintained that all history showed that capitalism was based upon force, however veiled, that it would finally defend its property rights against human rights by all necessary violence. Therefore he insisted that the only hope was violent revolution followed by a period of iron dictatorship. Since revolution always produces counter-revolution, they must use the ruthless methods of capitalism for its extinction: "From the first hour of victory, the workers must level their distrust against their former allies." Openly contemptuous of democracy as a bourgeois prejudice, reliance must be placed only upon a class-conscious minority. They must know neither compassion nor remorse but must forcibly terrorize their opponents into submission, "by execution, imprisonment, forced labor, control of the press. . . . Revolution is war and war is founded on terror." [1] Lenin says there can only be freedom when there are no classes, no surviving enemies, and when the state has finally disappeared.[2]

---

[1] *Karl Marx* by H. J. Laski, p. 36.

[2] "Only in Communist society . . . when the capitalists have disappeared, where there are no longer any classes . . . only then does the

Such is the theory and such the practice of communism. Let us notice how this dictatorship widens out to the control of almost all of life. For there is no halting place, nowhere to draw the line to limit its tendency to ubiquitous control. To begin with, a dictatorship must obviously dominate the entire government. But that is impossible without complete control of finance, of industry and of collective agriculture. All organizations such as trade unions and cooperatives must be brought into harmony with the general scheme. But since many of the older generation, undisciplined and untrained to the new order, prove recalcitrant or unresponsive, the rising generation must by all means be captured and molded. Therefore all of education, all pupils and students, and as quickly as possible, all teachers must be brought under the scheme of the dictatorship. They are concerned with what every teacher teaches and with what every pupil is taught. All education thus becomes propaganda.

All youth organizations must train for the new citizenship. But the control of formal education is not enough. All that the people read, all they see, all they are told must, as far as possible, be "truth" according to the dictatorship.

---

state disappear and can one speak of freedom." *The State and Revolution.* See *Liberty Under the Soviets,* p. 20.

Bukharin writes: "In extreme cases the workers' government must not hesitate to use the method of the terror. Only when the suppression of the exploiters is complete, when they have ceased to resist, when it is no longer in their power to injure the working class, will the proletarian dictatorship grow progressively milder. Meanwhile the bourgeoisie, little by little, will fuse with the proletariat; the workers' State will gradually die out; society as a whole will be transformed into a communist society in which there will be no classes." *A B C of Communism,* by N. Bukharin and E. Preobrazhensky, p. 81.

Therefore every radio, every moving picture, every newspaper and every line of the press must tell the same story, or permit only criticism by the proletarian class that does not attack the fundamental basis of the dictatorship.

But even this is not enough. Since all depends upon a party, *the* Party, the only one permitted, that above all must be united, "monolithic." It must present a "solid front" to its world of enemies. Therefore it is unsafe to allow complete democracy even within the one per cent of the population who are Party members. Any deviation to left or right, any continued criticism or independent action, after the supreme organ of authority has made its decision, is counted disloyalty and sedition and must be dealt with even more mercilessly than class enemies. Therefore the left wing sedition, Trotzky and several thousands of his followers, must be banished, exiled, imprisoned, excluded, silenced or crushed. No quarter can be given them in Russia or in any orthodox Communist Party in the world. And members in the deviation on the right, who think that the Party is moving too fast, and that the people are suffering from the strenuous pace, must be silenced or brought to their knees in repentance and humiliating confession.

Outside the Party, the dictatorship must so control that all who are counted class enemies of the regime must be crushed. For the most part they must not be allowed to leave the country which counts them "enemies", thus making Russia for them one vast prison house from which there is no escape. They are often denied work, or any means for their maintenance, refused a passport to leave the country, cut off from foreigners, suspected and hounded with spies if they have any intercourse whatever with them. Frequently prohibited from sending a penny of support to needy relatives outside the country, and often not allowed to receive help from them, they are a pitiful spectacle before the world. This applies not only to conservative White Russians but to all radicals and socialists who do not agree with communist orthodoxy as interpreted by the group in control of the central organs of the Party. Thus the dictatorship is extended largely to the control of nearly every individual in certain phases of life in Russia.

And let us notice not only how this dictatorship extends to almost the whole of life, but how the principal of "centralism" ever narrows the monopoly of power to the few. Theoretically, this is a dictatorship of the whole proletariat, all workers, peasants and soldiers or, let us say, nine-tenths of the population. But obviously this vast conglomeration of often uneducated, individualistic and potentially capitalistic peasants are not ready for effective membership in the proletariat. They must first turn to the industrial workers. But many of these also are not disciplined for a socialist society. Therefore the control must be practically limited to the Communist Party. But even this party is liable to a right or left "deviation" that is dangerous. Therefore the control must be centralized in an executive and then in a plenum of the executive. But since there are at least two fractions striving to dominate these bodies, one or the other must be excluded, and the loyal followers of the man or group in power must be placed in positions of authority.

Finally, the inner control narrows down to the nine members of a political bureau and their eight associates, and if any of these are not in harmony with one man and his associates they must be eliminated. Thus, in the end, a dictatorship of the whole working class or nine-tenths of the population, has a tendency to narrow itself to one man and a few loyal associates or followers who fill the interlocking positions of the secretariat, political and organization bureaus.

All of this is the natural and almost inevitable development of a dictatorship of the proletariat, which Lenin, loyally following Marx, defined to mean the "dictatorship of its determined and conscious minority."[1] It becomes in fact a minority, *very* determined, very conscious, and very small.

We have thus an ever-narrowing dictatorship in "democratic" centralism. What are its undesirable results? There is, first of all, the large liability of error for any minority which holds a dangerous monopoly of power. No man is infallible. A dictatorship must crush other minorities or individuals who oppose. It may at times even find itself in opposition to the majority or the great mass of the people, but *ex hypothesi*, it must "govern or get out." So it governs. Nearly all the reforms and hopes of history have been led at first by an opposing minority. But once action has been taken all such must be nipped in the bud. "It is a commonplace of history that power is poisonous to those who exercise it. . . . To sit continuously in the seat of office is inevitably to become separated from the minds and

---

[1] *Russian Soviet Republic,* p. 324.

wants of those over whom you govern. . . The special vice of every historic system of government has been its inevitable tendency to identify its own private good with the public welfare. To suggest that communists might do the same is no more than to postulate their humanity." [1]

Another possible result of such a dictatorship is the ever-present danger of tyranny by force. Such a system is usually bad both for rulers and ruled. Napoleon in the early idealism of the revolution presents something of a heroic figure, but in the end he appears a Corsican butcher who has reduced the physical and moral stature of the depleted manhood of France. Dictatorships are dangerous both to the dictator and to the dictated.

Once again, history repeats itself in the indefinite continuity of a dictatorship. It postulates its future millenium in a classless society where man shall not and cannot exploit his fellow man, where the state itself will "wither away" and men will do right from force of habit and early training in a favorable environment. But practically, within the limits of human experience, that time never comes. At least it never has come save in the utopian, incandescent imagination. Actually a dictatorship which was theoretically "temporary," must not only be indefinitely extended but ever-tightened and rendered more complete. It is true that the new environment created by the communist system largely eliminates the dangerous motivation of personal greed, which is the bane of western nations, but it begets a lust for power

---

[1] *Karl Marx*, p. 42, by H. J. Laski.

and a contempt for liberty and for individual personality that may prove as prolific a root of evil as the love of money.

Take the single instance of the denial of a free press. Concretely, what does this mean? What did it mean and what were its results in Czarist Russia? We may freely grant that this is for a whole class and for a higher end than Czarism, but what are the inevitable results of this method? Once you are determined to monopolize the press and to tell the people what you want them to believe about the virtues of your own government and the vices of every other, you must sustain a continuous system of propaganda that involves constant misrepresentation of foreign peoples and conditions.[1] To illustrate the evils of a controlled and kept press, it will be remembered that, side by side with a free England, Napoleon maintained his dictatorship in France. The news of Nelson's victory at Trafalgar and of Napoleon's defeat was not permitted publication in the French press for twelve years. Compare this with the Soviet Union today.

When the writer was in Russia in 1923 he was completely cut off from all foreign sources of world news. Suddenly on September first occurred the great Japanese earthquake. The author happened to be in the newspaper office of *Pravda,* or *Truth,* when the editor came up in great excitement to

---

[1] Professor Paul Monroe of Columbia, in a most sympathetic and appreciative monograph on Russian education, writes: "Constant misrepresentation of foreign peoples and conditions, misrepresentation of current events, and cultivation of enmity to foreign peoples, is, in my judgment, the one great blot on Russian education." *Observation on Present Day Russia,* Carnegie Series, No. 255, p. 588.

tell him the news.   There had, he said, been a terrific earthquake.   The bed of the ocean had been pushed up and an island had appeared above the surface of the sea.   And then the ships of the American navy steamed up and seized possession of this island, true to form, as the natural act of a wicked, imperialist and capitalist country.

It will be remembered that as a matter of fact the American ships were rushing supplies and relief to the victims of the earthquake.   But no such friendly cooperation could be admitted.   Only communist "truth," i. e., that which aids the revolution, must be told; while the wickedness of capitalist countries must be painted black.[1]   Think what it would mean to live under a regime where such a statement could not be contradicted or corrected.   As the communist leader well said: "People believe what they are told.   And we propose to tell them."   So they can if they wish.   And the followers of the Prophet in early Arabia, or of a primitive despotism or dictatorship will believe what they are told— for a time.   For a long time perhaps.   But, as Lincoln maintained, you cannot fool all the people all the time, and dictatorships often bring, not their prophesied millenium, but their own nemesis.   If truth is more precious than gold; if freedom for the mind is more priceless even than food for the body, who would voluntarily sell his liberties for such a dictatorship?   It might be forced upon an uneducated mass

---

[1] Joffe writes: "To deceive your class enemies, to violate, to destroy a treaty imposed by force, but never to sin against the revolutionary proletariat, never to violate the obligation taken on yourself before the revolution—those are the true revolutionary methods of the true revolutionary struggle."   *Izvestia,* Jan. 1, 1919.

unschooled in liberty, but will it ever appeal to the consent of a free people?

The aim of democracy is to produce "the capacity of continuous initiative" and the development of full personality by a government of, for and by all the people. Let us frankly grant that this ideal is as yet far from attainment on the part of liberalism. But what shall we say of dictatorship? If the outstanding evils of capitalism are its failure to provide equality, freedom and justice for the dispossessed mass, dependent on the few who own, or at least control, the means of production, how does dictatorship get beyond this so long as it denies so many of the essentials of liberty? Equally it begs the question to promise a future millenium when government has "withered away" on this earth, or to promise it in a future world as a compensation for injustice in the present. Even if the communist maintains that dictatorship is a temporary, necessary evil, at least it is an evil, stark and unmitigated, that he offers us. We repeat, it is a poor substitute for a Magna Carta seven centuries after a people have tasted the fruits of liberty.

An ever-tightening dictatorship that is always in danger of becoming, and sometimes does become, tyrannical breeds a continuous series of plots and counter-plots, real or imaginary.

Thus, in fear of the Baldwin cabinet and the die-hards in England in 1927 when relations were severed with Moscow, the Kremlin saw a deep, sinister purpose to overthrow Soviet Russia and Stalin wrote: "We refer not to some indefinite, vague 'danger' of a new war, but to the real and actual threat of a new war in general, and of a war against the Soviet Union in particular."[1] Following this a succession of incidents and situations served to maintain a continual war psychosis.

In August, 1930, a number of men were shot in Russia for hoarding silver change. In September forty-eight specialists of the meat packing industry were executed in connection with the discovery of a reported food plot. In November a plot was reported and indictments were drawn up against eight Russians held for trial in connection with an alleged world-wide conspiracy to start war against Soviet Russia. The public prosecutor, N. U. Krilenko, drew up an indictment in thirty solid newspaper columns against some forty-five persons at the center, 400 in the provinces, 1500 minor Russian adherents and many leading men in foreign countries, such as Sir Henry Deterding of the Royal Dutch Shell Oil Company in England. Self-admitted enemies, traitors and confessors, like Professor Ramsin, were reported to have divulged a plot to the effect that after a diplomatic "incident" on the Roumanian border, Roumania was to have declared war, to be followed in quick succession by Poland, France and England. An army of 600,000 men under General Loukomsky was to march on Moscow and another on Leningrad. France was to supply arms and ammunition and the British fleet was to steam into the Baltic and the Black Sea, attacking Leningrad and the Crimea.

It is quite natural that there should be plots, real or

---

[1] *Izvestia,* July 28, 1927.

imagined, where life is difficult under a high state of tension and where attacks are constantly launched by the group in power first against the left deviation of Trotzky, then against the ablest men on the right, who fear that the pace of the five year plan is too dangerously fast, like Premier Rykof, Tomsky and Bukharin.   It is to be expected that under such conditions there is often a factual basis for opposition or conspiracy; but also that there is a natural desire to find or to avail themselves of scapegoats who can be made to bear the brunt of blame for food shortage or hardships, or to keep the people diverted or keyed up on the defensive against some supposed approaching invasion from without or counter-revolution from within.   It is all quite natural and quite grim, but it hardly offers ground for believing that such a system is a final cure for humanity's social ills.

2. *World Revolution*

Here is our second indictment of the system: the dogma that the world can only be saved in one way, by the overthrow of the government in every capitalist country, when the time is ripe, through a destructive revolution of the Russian type, as insisted upon by Marx, Lenin and Stalin, iterated and reiterated unmistakably in all their writings.

Like dictatorship, revolution is to the communist an evil, but he counts it a necessary evil, caused and conditioned by the force which sustains the whole unjust capitalist order. Let us observe just what this doctrine of the inevitableness of revolution implies.   It is not merely a bloodless revolution, a swift *coup d'état* to enable the most wronged and benevolent class to seize the state and then all live happily ever afterward. Far from it. The whole process is a *"continuing revolution."* There is a long preparation, leading up to a transition, and followed by a permanent control, till one class only shall survive, and every individual who differs or opposes shall be obliterated, or, more euphemistically, "liquidated."

The American or French revolutions lasted a short time till each people was free from its oppressor and they had attained their measured objectives. Not so the continuing Russian revolution. That covers all of life and a vast period of time. It operates in at least three phases. First there is the period of preparation when the faithful communist individual and party is urged to be implacable in following out Lenin's twenty-one points adopted by the second congress of the Communist International in 1920, for "the revolutionary overthrow of capitalism." They are "obligated to proclaim a clear break with reformism and with the policy of the center and to propagate this break throughout the ranks of the entire party membership." Where this command is loyally carried out this means a split of hatred and division in every local trade union and every national labor movement in the world. In the labor movement, for instance, of Great Britain, or Germany, or Denmark contempt is poured upon every non-communist labor leader, and loyal communists are bidden to enter each movement in order to form factions for the purpose of weakening the authority of the recognized leaders and their adopted program. For illustration, the labor movement of France was relatively strong and effective for the cause of labor until it was weakened and divided by the communist split.

After the preparation there follows the second phase of the revolution itself. When the time is ripe, the state is to be seized by a determined minority and the whole process of the Russian Revolution repeated, allowing only for the variation of circumstances and details in other countries. The counter-revolution is to be put down by the terror, and the old system destroyed. We are not now pleading the merits or deserts of the capitalist state, but only pointing out the immeasurable risks of unlimited and uncontrollable destruction.

The third phase of the continuing revolution is the establishment of the dictatorship of the proletariat, with its ever-narrowing centralization of control, its ever-widening sphere of domination over each phase of life, and its ever-tightening grip until its last enemy has been abolished and in the classless society of the future, when no opposition remains, and no one wishes to continue in office or power it can safely "wither away." Such is the naïve credulity of its historically baseless future hope. The incorruptible bodies of the miracle-working saints of the Czarist church are easy to believe, as mere child's play of the religious fantasy, compared to the monstrous credulity involved in such a gratuitous promise. Under the alchemy of communism they are to sow dictatorship and reap liberty, to sow hate and reap love, to sow violence and destruction only to reap lasting peace and brotherhood ever afterward.

This policy of world revolution involves complete reliance on force, and the distrust of moral suasion and the principle of consent. It involves contempt for and enmity with all patient, evolutionary, constitutional, educational means and leaders who follow them, as "reformist," compromising and cowardly. Communism puts all its eggs in the one basket of destructive revolution and dictatorship. If it succeeds you have Russia. And if it fails? Imagination quails before the picture. And there can be no guarantee of success. Through war, revolution, famine and pestilence some ten millions perished in Russia between 1917 and 1921. The writer recalls the narrative of an eye-witness in the frozen famine region when corpses were eaten. But revolution in the scattered, rural population of Russia would be far less terrible than in a highly industrialized, dense population like that of Germany or England, largely dependent upon others for their food supply.[1]

In playing with revolution men are loosing the forces of

---

[1] Bukharin writes: "Many persons have supposed that the ferocious character of our civil war is due to the backwardness of our country, or to some peculiar 'Asiatic' traits. The opponents of revolution in western Europe are in the habit of saying that 'Asiatic socialism' flourishes in Russia, and that in 'civilised' lands a revolutionary change will be effected without atrocities. Obviously this is all nonsense. Where capitalist development is far advanced, the resistance of the bourgeoisie will be more stubborn. The intelligentsia (the professional classes, the technicians, the managing engineers, the army officers, etc.) are more strongly solidarised with capital, and are for that reason far more hostile to communism. In such countries, therefore, the civil war will inevitably assume a more savage form than in Russia. The course of the German revolution has actually proved that the war assumes harsher forms in countries where capitalist development is farther advanced." *A B C of Communism*, pp. 132–133.

the volcano, the earthquake or the forest fire, which no man nor centralized group can control. An individual may direct a bomb but he cannot limit a forest fire once it is lighted. However unorthodox and industrially undeveloped for revolution Russia may have been, perhaps never before in history was there such a favorable combination of a world war, a corrupt government, an indignant people and an able and ruthless leadership, such as met in Petrograd in 1917.

As Laski well observes: "We need not, as communism offers us, the formulæ of conflict, but the formulæ of co-operation. The sceptical observer is unconvinced that any system . . . is entitled from its certainties, to sacrifice all that has been acquired so painfully in the heritage of toleration and freedom, to the chance that its victory may one day compensate for a renunciation that on its own admission, is bound to be grim and long. . . He may suspect whether any regime that is built on hate and fear and violence can give birth to an order rooted in fraternity. For these create an environment of which the children are, equally, hate and fear and violence. The spirit of man ever takes its revenge for degradation inflicted upon it even in the name of good." [1]

The appeal to hate or fear or violence brings its own nemesis. A terror terrifies but it also paralyzes. The worst phases of the earlier Cheka have of course passed, but the appeal to fear is still utilized. For illustration, suppose an engineer in Russia makes a mistake. Perhaps through no fault of his own his bridge, or irrigation dam or factory

---

[1] H. J. Laski, *Communism,* p. 244.

does not succeed. He may be tried for sabotage and imprisoned. Immediately fear takes hold upon others. They hesitate to take responsibility. Spies are everywhere. Russia has always believed in them, rather than in freedom. Unexpectedly, swiftly the lightning strikes, or the blow falls upon the unfortunate. There is an arrest at midnight. No counsel or witness is allowed in the secret trial of the G. P. U. A nameless terror broods and settles down like a cloud. That is why many who would otherwise do so are unable to do their best work under such a system. That is why many a tourist feels a sense of release, as of a burden or a cloud lifted, when he leaves a land that believes in dictatorship, in force and in fear.

Bertrand Russell points out two objections to the communist doctrine of violence: "Once the principle of respecting majorities as expressed at the ballot-box is abandoned, there is no reason to suppose that victory will be secured by the particular minority to which one happens to belong. There are many minorities beside communists: religious minorities, teetotal minorities, militarist minorities, capitalist minorities. . . . They believe that communism is for the good of the majority; they ought to believe that they can persuade the majority on this question, and to have the patience to set about the task of winning by propaganda. . . .

"The second argument of principle against the method of minority violence is that abandonment of law, when it becomes widespread, lets loose the wild beast, and gives a free reign to the primitive lusts and egoisms which civilization in some degree curbs. . . . Civilization is not so stable that it cannot be broken up; and a condition of lawless violence is not one out of which any good thing is likely to emerge. . . . The Bolshevik philosophy is promoted very largely by despair of more gradual methods. But this despair is a mark of impatience, and is by no means warranted by the facts." [1]

Creativity and construction, at their best, often depend upon the motivation of love. Revolution and destruction, at their worst, await the kindling fire of hate. Biologically and sociologically, love involves creation and sharing, while hatred is primarily destructive. It has murder at its heart. Perhaps it is the murder of wrong and in the face of flagrant and entrenched social evil, it may be closely akin to moral indignation. But if love is blind, hatred moves in darkness. According to the communist slogan: "Revolution is a storm sweeping aside everything that stands in its path"—good as well as evil. It may be swift and strong to destroy, but powerless to build again in the midst of its ashes and embers of ruin. Here is a promised panacea, and it must be judged upon its merits and by its final results. Its mandate is: "Destroy all opposition, hate your enemies, overcome evil with evil, and good will result."

But there is another and opposing principle in life. Its commandment is: "Love even your enemies, overcome evil with good, beget the good that you would seek by creative love, believe in men and in their ultimate response to moral suasion, trust them and appeal to the consent of the governed rather than coerce them by violence; patience can yet create a classless brotherhood by faith and hope and love."

[1] *Bolshevism in Theory and Practice,* pp. 146–149.

Communists would tell us that these are baseless dreams, that free men will never love or share or give justice to their dispossessed dependents. If that is so, if those who have power flaunt their unshared wealth in the face of unrelieved poverty and want and unemployment, then red history as written in Russia will repeat itself. Communists will in time apply their principles if we decline to apply ours. If we refuse to give justice they will take by violence; if we refuse to share in love, they will destroy in hate. It may be a race between education and catastrophe, between quickened evolution and destructive revolution, between frankly declared principles applied in a program of action or the fate of Bourbons, Hohenzollerns, Romanoffs and profiteers the world over.

3. *Intolerant Persecution.*

Communism is a dogma. It seems to hold inevitably an element of bigotry, of intolerance, and of fanaticism implicit in it. It does not seem to spring primarily from the discovery of some great, positive truth which makes its way by its own irresistible appeal and can freely win the consent of majorities. Rather it originated from a counsel of despair, a negative conclusion that truth cannot win its way by moral suasion alone, but that a "determined minority" who have accepted the dogma must seize power by force, must never relinquish it until their last enemy is extinguished, and must impose their dictatorship upon all others. We may grant the benevolent intentions of a Moslem, a fascist or a communist dictatorship and that there are some good results in each. But the question is—What price dictatorship? Is it necessarily at the cost of a harsh intolerance? The dogma of communism is akin, not to the enlightenment of a Gautama, the good news of Christ, or the moral suasion of a Gandhi, but to the sword of Islam, which offers only the alternatives of submission, tribute or death.

This intolerance springs necessarily from the negative philosophy of Marx himself. Marx, for all his giant intellect and indomitable spirit, was unable to grasp the full significance of our complex world. By an over-simplification, all history is ultimately forced into the arbitrary channels of two classes and their inevitable conflict. The seven-fold rainbow of reality is reduced to stark black and white, and men are divided into the two simple classes of robbers and robbed, exploiters and exploited. Allowing only for the element of time and development in the process of history, the multiform possibilities of experimental solutions are impatiently swept away and one panacea is substituted which is to have universal significance, whether finally in Thibet or immediately in Great Britain. They teach that all any country needs ultimately is a proletarian revolution. All history is based on a single materialist foundation; all economics on a simple theory of labor and surplus value, all strategy is reduced to the class war, and all liberty narrowed to a dictatorship. The panacea is simplicity itself. Marx, Lenin and Stalin are all examples of the incarnation of this dogma, and of the price that has to be paid for it.

We do not deny that there is a certain element of the heroic in the old Jewish prophet championing the cause of the disinherited toilers of the world and hurling his invectives against a whole capitalist world of oppressors; nor in Lenin with his back to the wall and his life in his hand facing the hungry mob on the gun carriage in Petrograd, demanding a people's revolution; nor in Stalin and a handful of leaders striving to build a workers' republic with a whole world against them. There is an element of heroism but also of harshness, of strength coupled with intolerance, of courage manifested in fanatical bigotry, in each of the three men and in their resultant system of society.

Marx felt, as had the prophets of his race before him, a deep identification with the *economic* needs of humanity about him. Here he was a prophet of judgment. But there were whole areas of experience to which he was stranger. Religion, for instance, he could never understand nor appreciate. His life, heroic as it was in many respects, was lived too largely in the abstractions of the library of the British Museum. He was an isolated stranger largely out of touch even with the British working men about him. His view of human nature is abstract and over-simplified, his interpretation of history, after its preliminary stages have been fulfilled according to a simple pattern, is as we have seen, artificially narrowed to a single class conflict and a single panacea, which is to be imposed upon the world by blood and iron. Doubtless a "Christian" Chancellor and Hohenzollern monarch drove him as a hunted exile to the conclusion that state and church were both necessary enemies of the people, and that they must be ruthlessly destroyed before a workers' government could build upon their ashes.

But natural and explicable as his negative conclusion was, Marx was unable to grasp the complex reality of the concrete world, and, in consequence, communism fails to this day to grasp it.   A narrow dogmatism is the result.   The overtones and softer shades of life are lost in Soviet Russia. A thousand values are swept away with a contemptuous gesture as "bourgeois prejudice."   Just as the leader of the Huns could sack Rome and the stern conqueror of Islam could watch the burning treasures of the library at Alexandria, both unmoved because to their simplified dogma other values were meaningless, so they are today before the hard and narrow materialistic dogma of Marxism.[1]

Moscow hates the word religion like a bad dream and may seek in the end to destroy what seems to them only a reactionary superstition from life.   It adopts a materialistic religion of industrialization and makes the machine its god. Any dogmatic religion in its early stages asks no questions and allows none.   It preaches a crusade.   It tolerates no rivals nor enemies.   It may build perhaps a robot world. Time only can tell.   That in itself would not be so intolerable if its harsh dogma would permit others to build their individual or social life according to their own patterns and values.   But there are no other values save their own that such a dictatorship of a single dogma can see or admit.   And

---

[1] As John Dewey says: "Marx had no conception, moreover, of the capacity of expanding industry to develop new inventions so as to develop new wants, new forms of wealth, new occupations; nor did he imagine that the intellectual ability of the employing class would be equal to seeing the need for sustaining consuming power by high wages in order to keep up production and its profits." *Individualism Old and New,* p. 103.

this means tragedy for all who differ, who are conceived as enemies, imprisoned within the iron bars of a dictatorship which permits no escape. And it is tragedy for a divided world, separated not only geographically between two conflicting social orders, but often between members of the same family, who speak two different languages and live in two worlds, the poles apart, divided between those who do and those who do not submit to the Islam of the Marxian dogma.

The harsh dogmatism of communism shows itself in their intolerant propaganda against all whom they regard as their class enemies, whether within or without Russia. Breaking up meetings seems to be a favorite indoor sport. Boring from within and wrecking if they cannot capture trade unions seems to be an established policy. The creation of class hatred is a major endeavor. They seem particularly bitter against liberals, radicals or socialists who differ from them, such as Ramsay MacDonald or Norman Thomas.

As typical of their line of attack we give a single illustration. In the recent troubles in our Southern textile mills the American Civil Liberties Union generously furnished bail of $30,000 for a group of persecuted communist workers. These men "jumped" their bail and left for Moscow, where they remained with the approval of the Party. This act came close to closing the door for bail in future cases of a similar sort. Judges now have an excuse for fixing very high bail, and even sympathetic friends will be afraid to risk the amount involved. Hence the Civil Liberties Union felt obliged to refrain from trying to raise bail in similar cases in the future. Without the slightest evidence of gratitude or acknowledgment of help given, the following communist press release thus bitterly assails those who had sought to defend them, attacking them with seemingly malicious falsehood, for not one of the five sentences of the indictment is true: "Norman Thomas, the social fascist candidate of the Socialist Party, who was present in the chambers when the massacre took place, (reference is to police brutality to the leader of a Communist Delegation to the Board of Estimate) smiled charmingly in true ministerial fashion.[1] Only last week Thomas led the attack within the executive committee of the American Civil Liberties Union against imprisoned and tortured workers by refusing them bail and attacking the International Labor Defense in its defense of militant jailed workers in the present economic crisis. The answer to the cry for bread is billies. On this, the Republican, Socialist, and Democratic Parties are one. The Rev. Norman Thomas and Mayor Walker are the direct representatives of capitalist America against the bitter struggle for work or wages."[2]

Such propaganda may appeal to ignorant workers un-

---

[1] Sam Nessin, leader of the communist delegation, continued a protest to the point of breaking up the meeting. He was ordered out of the room by the Mayor who, however, indulged in cheap talk about fighting him if he (the Mayor) were not presiding at the meeting. This probably encouraged the police, who needed no encouragement, to beat up Nessin very badly, not in the Hall of the Board of Estimate, but downstairs. Norman Thomas was present at the meeting, he did not smile, and as soon as he knew of the beating, which was only after it occurred, he protested most vigorously.

[2] Quoted in *The World Tomorrow,* November, 1930.

acquainted with the facts in a country where the whole press is completely controlled as in Russia, but it will never commend itself or appeal to the intelligence of free men in a country where the press is not gagged.   It is to be hoped that the day will come when the communists themselves will see that such propaganda is shortsighted and self-defeating. It is as filthy as it is false.   But, unfortunately, it is all too typical of the communist press today in Russia, in the United States and in other lands.   It illustrates the harsh dogmatism of communism.

The intolerant dogmatism of the communist position manifests itself in almost every area and relationship of life.   It has a different conception of the value of human life, of the worth of personality or the rights of the individual.   While the writer was in Moscow recently a number of men were shot for hoarding silver change, to the value of twenty-five dollars or more.   It is true that this had become a menace to their currency system and to social welfare.   In speaking of this to a communist professor he replied in substance: "Did we shoot them?   Of course, why not?   There were four mentioned today you say?   I am only surprised that there were so few.   Would you think that the report of four killed in a battle in your World War would be surprising? You do not realize that we are now at war.   We shall kill all that we must to win this war."   This man was a professor, a man of learning.   On his shelves were many religious books as he was an expert on the history of religions. He was inflexibly honest, self-sacrificing, loyal to humanity in the mass, if they belonged to the proletarian class.   Yet he thought no more of shooting four men or forty-eight men later in the "food plot," than he would of killing that many cockroaches on his floor. Of course he would not like to do either, for he is a gentleman and a scholar, and killing cockroaches or men would be unesthetic and unpleasant, at best a regrettable necessity.[1] Unfortunately, we cannot appeal to a visitant from Mars to judge between these two views of life. But to members of the western world of liberalism, the manifold results of such an intolerant dogmatism are appalling. They are devastating alike to living a free, or complex, or abundant life with any deviation from orthodoxy within the confines of the dictatorship, save on its prescribed terms, or to understanding or cooperation with the world outside.

Nowhere is this more apparent than in the sphere of religion. To this dogmatism, religion is superstition, religion is opium, religion is poison. Marx and Lenin both declared it to be so. Therefore the case is closed. We are told repeatedly by educated men in Russia that "every true scientist is an atheist." If there is any question about it, a quotation from Marx or Lenin will settle it. It is vain to say we believe in science and evolution as much as they, that so many of the great scientists from Kepler and Newton to our own day were believers. It is useless to point out that Darwin, according to his own autobiography, was a reverent agnostic. All that is meaningless and valueless. Under

---

[1] The writer believes he is not doing this man an injustice for he is sending this manuscript, including this section of it, for his correction and criticism.

such an artificially simplified dogma the individual is black or white, theist or atheist, capitalist or communist, comrade or enemy. Within the dictatorship it must be submission or spiritual death.

The communist does not see that though he repudiates the word religion, he has himself set up a new fanatical religion of atheistic humanism. Professor Ross speaks of "the terrible single-mindedness of the fanatic." It makes a difference whether this is an academic phrase written at safe distance, or a solid fact within the confines of the terror. There is a certain undeniable gain in simplicity, in the strength of dogmatism, in the enthusiasm of an unthinking crusade. But there is also appalling loss. The flaming theism of Islam and atheism of communism present a strange parallel. Either may conquer us with force, but they will not win our consent until they can appeal to reason. And it is difficult to see how either can do that without such radical alteration that they would lose not only their force, but their distinctive identity.

It is to be regretted that our very difference of vocabulary leads to conflict and misunderstanding. The communist loathes "religion." But what is religion? Suppose that, reduced to its simplest terms it were conceived as the effort to bring the whole life into the light of the best that we know, and then to live our life in loyalty to that best. Suppose that, with Reinhold Niebuhr, we think of religion at a minimum as faith in something that reason cannot justify, and at the maximum as the belief that the universe backs that faith. Although of course such terminology would satisfy neither the fundamentalist theist nor atheist, yet upon any such broad definition, Southern Buddhism, though atheistic, is a religion, and communism is likewise a fanatical, materialist, atheistic religion. Large numbers of independent observers have been impressed with this fact.

But let us pass from definition to life. Whenever man has been left free as he passes from the primitive to the higher reaches of civilization, he always responds to his environment in at least three ways in science, in art, in religion. In science he seeks to master and control his environment and improve his life; in art to beautify, to harmonize and enrich it; in religion to integrate, to unify, to relate his life to its spiritual source within and to its ends without. From Plato, from Hegel, the teacher of Marx, to Woodrow Wilson, men have pointed out the values in religion, both individual and social, as a great architectonic force in life. Multitudes of men have experienced these values and would die for them. All would admit the caricatures, the perversions, the miscarriages that history records in religion as well as in science, in art, in politics and every other field of life. But what is the remedy? Communism says there is only one. Destroy and rebuild according to the dogma and the dictatorship of a proletarian state.

It is one thing for Marx to propose this on paper. It is quite another to embody this in flesh and blood. When the writer was telling the Russian emigrés in Paris of the possibilities of a great world's laboratory of social experiment, one of them replied in substance: "A laboratory is a fine thing in theory. But suppose your own family and

your own relatives are in the crucible. Suppose that fifty
of your relatives and friends were shot by the Cheka or perished in the revolution, the terror and the civil war that followed. Suppose that many of your friends were now in
poverty, not allowed to leave the country, hounded with
spies, some of them in exile for their religion, do you think
you would be so enthusiastic about this laboratory?"

And here is our final indictment of the system. As we
have seen, they tolerate religion to the extent of still permitting worship in the majority of the churches. But many
are in exile, some are persecuted for their religion, and the
leaders frankly state that they intend to do all in their
power finally "to liquidate this superstition," to extirpate
this poisonous growth from the human heart. And here, in
sympathy at least, we are all in their crucible. Our civil
liberties, our religious freedom, our tolerance, our liberalism, our whole complex of priceless values, which the coarse
thumb and finger of a materialistic dogmatism fail to feel—
nearly all we most value in life is at stake.

Communists will claim that they are not persecuting religion, as did the high official previously referred to. But
we would reply as we did to him that they certainly are doing so. The writer could name whole sectarian denomina-
tions that have suffered severely and are still suffering from
persecution.

The writer will confine himself to a single illustration.
There is a certain body in Russia held in high regard
throughout the world, though they are now isolated and,
without foreign connections, who neither ask nor receive help

from abroad.   A number of them had their own communal farms, happily and successfully, long before the October Revolution.   But although enonomically collectivized, their land was taken from them and given to others.   Cut off from their natural means of livelihood and the free expression of their religious views, they asked to be allowed to leave the country.   They authorized the writer to ask the proper authority if they might be permitted to emigrate to Canada, there to establish their own collective or communal farms, going out empty handed save for their few personal effects, and taking not a cent of money with them.   This was absolutely refused.   It will be remembered how the Germans in 1929, once prosperous, but with most of their property expropriated and persecuted for their religion, left in desperation, after President Hindenburg and others had generously subscribed to relieve their distress.   The indignant Swedes left likewise.   But others are no longer allowed to leave.   Not only have they been refused permission to leave but some of them today are on the terrible Solovyetzky Island.   They desire no publicity.   No people on earth are more ready bravely and silently to suffer.   In other lands, a place where one is forcibly detained is called a prison. Russia is just that for a multitude today, however much they are in the minority.   We repeat that the whole system for the long-oppressed proletarian majority has economically meant release, creative expression, substantial betterment. But for some millions of the minority, it is a prison house from which there is no escape.   Such a thing, after the revelations of George Kennan and others concerning the

Siberian exiles of the Czar, we called damnable. And, calling a spade a spade, such a thing we call damnable today. That which is a terror to such a large minority in Russia today is odious to the whole world.

This then is our threefold indictment of the Soviet system: a dictatorship that extends to almost all of life, and that takes the form sometimes of tyranny and sometimes of terror; the policy of world revolution by violence as the only panacea of social deliverance; and the intolerance, bigotry and persecution which spring from the Marxian dogma of communism.

CHAPTER XI

Let us pass from the duty of negative criticism to the more constructive task of appreciation. We must not let the evils of the system blind us to its values nor prejudice us against its merits. For, like capitalist countries, Russia is a vast complex, a mixture of good and evil. In the opinion of the writer, the Russian Revolution is like the French Revolution writ large and extended to the whole of life. Greater evil will probably result from it than from the Revolution in France, as has already been the case, for instance, in China. But far greater good also, in our judgment, may eventuate from it than even from the liberty, equality and fraternity of Republican France.

If, in spite of all these evils as they appear to us, with almost the whole world against them, and compelled to ask their followers for such constant privation and sacrifice, there is not only such persistence and power of survival in the system, but such enthusiasm for it on the part of so many within and without Russia, it must be because it stands for something of permanent worth. "The French Revolution lit flames in the hearts of mankind which, because it responded to something fundamental in human nature neither its errors nor its crimes could quench." And this is even more true of the Russian Revolution. Throughout the whole world and the whole of human history, men have prevailingly seen the scales of injustice tipped against the masses in favor of the classes.   Here at last is a promise of redress for the majority.   Here is something that is their own.   It was conceived and constructed for them, and in their opinion it is a system of and by and for the workers. The positive affirmations of communism may prove to be more essential than its denials; the ends it seeks more important than the methods by which it seeks them.   There is always a certain splendor in the stern renunciation and heroic appeal of a great crusade, especially if its goal is not the possession of an empty tomb but of a living humanity. Garibaldi's offer of cold and hunger and rags has always been irresistible if made by trusted leaders for a worthy goal.   "Communism has made its way by its idealism and not its realism, by its spiritual promise, not its materialistic prospect.   It is a creed in which there is intellectual error, moral blindness, social perversity.   Religions make their way despite these things." [1]   What power must lie, for instance, in a system that could survive the corruptions of a Constantine, the butchery of crusades, the cruelty of inquisitions, the opposition to science, the suppression of social reform, and prostitution to autocratic states as in Czarist Russia that have characterized Christianity at its worst! What good must lie in the heart of an iconoclasm that could yet bless the world after its regicide, its guillotine and its red terror, as in France!   The same is true in Russia.

---

[1] *Communism,* by H. J. Laski, p. 250.

Space will only permit the discussion of three possible values in the Russian system.

1. *The Passion for Social Justice*

There is a willingness on the part of the leaders to live the simple life of sacrificial sharing, with the consequent enthusiasm of large numbers of the working masses for the whole system and its arduous programs. It is a familiar spectacle to see a party in power lining its own nest and weakened by selfish corruption and luxury. The fallen empires rotted from the top; their leaders betrayed their people. Here, for almost the first time in history upon such a scale, we have the leaders of a whole nation, and that the largest in the world, sharing wellnigh all that they have with the people. All of property, of profit, of income; all of culture, of music, of art; all of leisure, of recreation, of enjoyment— all that they have, save power perhaps, is shared. Instead of asking special privileges, they impose upon themselves unusual sacrifices. Instead of demanding special leniency they demand the heaviest penalties upon Party members. Unlike the political boss or party politician, instead of the lion's share of the material spoils, they prescribe a "party maximum" of 225 roubles a month or $3.75 a day.[1] A few are allowed certain royalties on their writings, for instance, but have to return one-quarter or more of such meager allowances to the general funds. They must respond to endless subscriptions, demands and appeals for fellow sufferers

---

[1] In Moscow the party maximum is 300 roubles a month or about $5.00 a day. In less expensive centers it is lower.

or comrades all over the world.   The whole scheme involves incessant communal sharing.

They must not only work unsparingly at their daily task, but give evenings and long hours of unrequited service to countless committees, meetings and organizations.   They must face the frequent Party "cleansing" to give an account of their stewardship and prove their constant and loyal allegiance.   In the factories non-Party workers are asked to testify against any members of the Party who have been merely looking out for their own interests and not serving all the workers.   We can hardly imagine such a purge of political parties and politicians in the West.

The higher officials have, of course, their apartments provided, though they are often limited in space.   Automobiles are furnished for their professional service, though not for "joy riding."   But the sons of the poor peasants and workers are often admitted to the universities and to other privileges before those of Party members and officials.

Even the President, Kalinin, must live the simple life in his flannel shirt.   Stories of luxury and extravagance on the part of the leaders are for the most part grossly false. Officials engaging in "revelry" and graft such as that of the Ohio gang during President Harding's administration, would, after a fair public trial, be publicly shot.   Probably no officials or political leaders in the world, apart from Gandhi and his followers, so uniformly live the strenuous and simple life of self-denial.   When one contrasts a system of liberalism which produces its capitalist type blind to poverty and human need, its gang warfare, bootlegging, lawlessness, graft, corruption, greed and social injustice, one needs must pause before casting the first stone at the undoubted evils of communism. If we are told that it is really not a workers' state but only the rule of a small oligarchy, we are reminded of former Ambassador Girard's original list of the fifty-eight men who are said to rule America. They are practically all men of great wealth. That is the source of their power. We are told that they have not time to accept office themselves but that they determine who shall do so.

Whatever its evils, the system of Russia as a whole gets beyond the motive of private greed and the rule of wealth. It stands for communal sharing. No Christian could object to this in principle, as in the voluntary sharing of the early church that held "all things common." [1]

The communists do not stand for an academic, rigid equality, but for general sharing. They recognize that there are differences of talents and of service. But on the whole they more nearly approximate equality than any large political body in history. Lenin, working sixteen hours a day, lived in a small and relatively bare room, with workingman's food and clothing, upon two or three dollars a day. The technician or engineer who is subordinate to the Party member in a factory may be receiving several hundred dollars a month, while the communist over him may receive less than half as much.

This passion for justice, this almost puritan simplicity

---

[1] *Acts* 2:44, 4:32-35.

and at times asceticism, this demand for sharing and essential equality is not only practiced by the leaders, but to a large extent permeates the workers and is passed on with even increased intensity to the youth organizations. It is remarkable how, more than thirteen years after the revolution, they are able not only to perpetuate but at times even to increase this spirit. Other movements have lost their primitive simplicity and have grown rich and soft, but the central principle of this system, its passion for social justice, makes the individual profiteer a public disgrace and a scandal. He becomes a moral leper. The goal of ambition always placed before youth is not only social service, but a militant crusade which shall make this system triumphant in a world of greed. Every loyal youth is knit in sympathy and endeavor into the cause of the liberation of the workers of the world. In what other system are children in common schools taught to adjust their daily habits and their life's ambition to the neediest class of a common humanity throughout the entire world? Even Gautama's renunciation never made such imperative demands upon the common man. Garibaldi's privileged "thousand" is multipled to the million, with both a personal and a mass appeal that is terrific, not to free one's country from a foreign invader, but to save a whole world from its oppressors.

For the most part the leaders under the soviet system are honest, hard-working, self-denying and able men. However he may differ from them in principle, no one can read impartially the life of Marx, of Lenin or of Stalin, without admitting their courage and sacrifice. The same is true of most of the high officials in Russia today. Typical of the small group of the old nobility who have entered the Party and the Government, is a former prince. In our interview with **him we found** him equally ready to converse with us in Russian, German, French, Italian or English. On the whole, we chose English! His family is older than that of the Romanov Czars. The wide acres of his family's former vast estates, which are now occupied by successful peasants' collectives, were suggestive of the change in his own life.

As a member of the old regime of special privilege now serving efficiently and whole-heartedly in a workers' republic, we asked him among others two questions: "How can you, with your past special privileges be content to work for the party maximum of two hundred and twenty-five roubles a month, or $3.75 a day, which is less than an unskilled worker would get in the Ford Motor Works? And how can you, as a gentleman, a man apparently of humane consideration for your fellow-men, support a policy of world revolution? To put it bluntly, why do you communists want to kill people?"

His answer was substantially as follows: "You ask why I should be content with such a meagre income? But why should I not be? All my wants are provided for. I have three ample meals a day. More would make me ill. I can wear but one suit of clothes at a time. I have an excellent roof over my head and no discomforts of which to complain. But suppose I had. What satisfaction can the amassing of money or mere private profit give? Why should such a cheap and ignoble pursuit even interest us? We are building not only a new Russia, in contrast to the old order, but a new world. We seek a world of justice for the workers and the release of their creative energies. Is that not a worthier goal, a more thrilling adventure, a deeper satisfaction? Certainly it is for me.

"But you ask: Why do we want to kill people? Do you really mean that such is your conception of our system? I am sorry that there were some people killed in our Revolution. They were relatively few for it was almost a bloodless conflict until the outbreak of counter-revolution, the sabotage of the old classes of privilege, Allied intervention and the invasion of our country. If I remember rightly, there were some people killed in your own American Revolution which lasted for seven years after 1776. I am sorry, but people have a way of being killed in revolutions. I suppose it is a necessary evil.

"The skilful surgeon who performs a dangerous operation at the risk of life and often with the certainty of giving pain, does not do this because he wants 'to kill people' or to cause suffering. He is trying to save life and he knows of no other way, in the last resort, than a dangerous and painful surgical operation. So it is with revolution. We know of no other way, for all other ways have failed. They failed in Russia after four hundred years of Czarism. They are failing still in the continued social injustice after all these centuries in your capitalistic countries.

"And you seriously think that we want to kill people? Frankly, we thought that you were the killers. Take your recurring capitalist and imperialist wars; your world war, your pestilential slums. Do you know the death rate in the slums of your own city of New York? I was in America investigating. I have written a book upon it. Think of the more than six hundred thousand darkened tenement rooms of your city, where your slums continue, generation after generation, in tenements, many of them long ago condemned as unfit for human habitation. And yet you go on profiteering out of them just as we did in Czarist Russia. And you will never destroy them. You will never give them justice any more than we did in old Russia. How many little children are you killing, with your high death rate in your slums, decade after decade?

"And, take again your World War. How many did you kill? Was it ten million young men at the front? Did not Russia alone lose more than three millions? And how about the non-combatants? Add the women and children, and all told was it not twenty-six millions that was your death roll? Compare with that the handful killed in our Revolution during a few days of street fighting, until the capitalist world and the imperialist nations invaded our country to back up the forces of the reactionary Czarist regime that were against a workers' republic. In the light of all these facts, can you seriously talk of our wanting to kill people? No, we believe that a swift surgical operation, even though necessarily at the risk of some loss of life and of pain, will actually save life, compared to the continuing slums with their high death rate, the widespread unemployment, the inevitable and recurring wars of competitive capi-

talism and conquering imperialism.   In the light of all the
facts I would ask, who are the killers, you or we?   Neither
of us want to kill people.   But, I repeat, who is doing so
to-day, you or we?"

2. *A Classless Society*

A second value in the system would seem to be the principle of relative equality, the measurable advance toward
the goal of a classless society, with the absence of racial and
color prejudice.

Always excepting their class enemies, the principle of
human equality runs through the whole system.   It seems
to make no difference whether a man is white or black,
yellow or brown; whether a worker is a man or a woman.
There must be equal pay for equal work.   All offices must
be open to all.   All laws, all privileges must be equal.   In
no country in the world do women occupy so many positions of importance.   With pogroms long fomented by
Czarist police, or state, or church, prejudice against the Jew
still lingers in some quarters.   But the principle of the
system, the laws of the state, the practices and propaganda
of the Communist Party are doing all that can be done
to lessen and finally eliminate this evil.   Jews never had a
monopoly of power in the soviet system as reported by
foreign propaganda.   No full member of the inner Political Bureau is at present a Jew.   Yet there is probably no
country where Jewish citizens of real ability are allowed
without prejudice to occupy so many positions of importance.

In a world among whose major problems race prejudice bulks so large, it may make a real contribution to find one system which so transcends this prejudice. In the world today probably four peoples suffer most from this disease of race and color prejudice, the Americans, the British, the Germans and the high caste people of India in their attitude toward and treatment of the "untouchable" outcaste. No people has achieved a greater racial equality than the Russians and no system better promotes it than theirs. With nearly two hundred different nationalities, their treatment of their minorities and their granting of political, cultural and educational autonomy to each little "republic," has been as remarkable as was their persecution under the previous Czarist regime.

The soviet system precludes a foreign imperialism that would conquer nations from without by military conquest and rule peoples against their will as in India, the Philippines, or Korea. Doubtless they would not consistently fulfill their promise of permitting voluntary withdrawal from the U. S. S. R. union, but would try at all costs to hold a republic like Georgia within the federation, as the United States did the seceding South. They will as frankly encourage and aid national revolutions everywhere as did France in the American Colonies in 1776. But their treatment of oriental or African races upon a basis of absolute equality is in striking contrast to some Christian nations. The Tartar or the Slav can be cruel, but lynching as a manifestation of racial prejudice would be unthinkable under their system. To make radically different educational appropriations for white and black children, as in so many North American states, to permit legal or economic injustice on racial grounds, to deny the ballot to men because of their color would never be tolerated under a system where the term "comrade" covers a more real equality than does the term "brotherhood" in Anglo-Saxon countries.   It does not take much imagination to see how this principle of equality may in time appeal to every race, or colony, or possession that feels itself conquered or oppressed.   Perhaps the searchlight of such a disquietingly challenging system may well be turned upon the evils, the inconsistencies and the hypocrisies of older and more complacent systems, if the idealism of their own religion and democracy fails to move them.   We are not done with Russia yet.   No exclusion or blockade, no refusal of recognition, no false propaganda against them can prevent this searchlight being turned full upon the glaring social evils of our own system, or upon theirs.

3. *A World Laboratory of Social Experiment*

By a system of trial and error, under a relentless realism, vast experiments may be tried in Russia that may prove of great significance for the world.   Some other systems are set like cement in changeless forms.   They are ossified, petrified, stiff with conservatism.   White-hot, the molten metal of this new order seems to run swiftly into fresh molds and lend itself to new forms.   There is an openness, an experimental daring, an elasticity and freedom, save where these are precluded by their economic dogma.

It is probable that some of their experiments will fail and some will succeed, but both may be useful. For illustration, the communists tried workmen's control of factories in a sudden and almost complete industrial democracy. Its failure was as consistent as it was complete. They learned their lesson. Never again must labor be allowed a monopoly of power, and never again on the other hand must it be subjected to an external monopoly of autocratic control. They quickly learned in a costly experiment, which other countries were not free to try, that both were disastrous.

Russia is bold in these experiments. Her whole life is in the melting pot. All precedents, all propriety, all prejudice; all laws, all customs, all methods—anything and everything must be scrapped if they can discover a better way. Perhaps most of the discoveries of the race have been made in the laboratory of the scientist or in the larger school of life and practical experience. Russia values both, but especially the second. No other system ever so staked its very existence upon faith in the common man.

From among many in various fields we may recall several experiments which have already been mentioned that are of great possible significance for Russia herself and for the world, such as the five year plan, collective farming and socialization of all of life.

The five year plan, as we have observed, is probably the boldest economic experiment in the world today. If, out of chaos, anarchy and ruin, without foreign loans, and in the face of a world economic depression and of world opposition a backward and poor people can increase their production in agriculture over 50 per cent, in light industry 200 per cent, in heavy industry 300 per cent, and in electric power some 400 per cent, what may they not accomplish? Some countries face a "labor problem" of strikes and the obstruction of organized labor in conflict with the interests of those who own and profit by the means of production. What may not be possible if this vast body of opposing wage earners become themselves the owners, the inventors, the enthusiastic initiators of a great common advance of industry for what they conceive to be the emancipation of the workers of the world? A united cooperative crusade may accomplish what the conflicts and competition of class strife cannot. A five year period will obviously be only the first milestone of a long-distance race between the two systems and principles. Not the dogmatic propaganda of the printing press but the solid results of the industrial laboratory must decide between the two.

Collective agriculture, cooperative and industrialized farming is another major experiment in this world laboratory. From ancient times the farmer, though the basic producer, has been a problem. The pagan of the field, the heathen of the heath, the peasant in his distant isolation, the individualistic farmer—none of these have yielded to the more rapid civilization and socialization of urban life. To no system was the individualistic peasant a greater menace than in Russia. None blocked the social advance more than the closed individual "fist" of the *kulak* profiteer. Yet suddenly, within five years this basis of loose sand is being united into what may prove to be the reinforced concrete of a bed-rock foundation for the whole social system.

Outside of India and China, which are relatively static and paralyzed by caste or custom of religious and social systems, here is the largest rural population in the world. One new tractor or combine may perform the work of more than fifty men with the medieval plow, hand sickle and flail. Within a decade or two, at the present rate, Russia may be the largest producer of grain, and perhaps of tractors, in the world. And she is socializing as rapidly as she is industrializing her agriculture. Little Denmark has shown the possibilities during recent years of cooperation in a tiny country. What may not giant Russia do in the next two decades? And, quite apart from the theory of a particular academic system, and without any connection with communism, may there be possible lessons in this for America, Canada, Australia, India or China? Since the industrial revolution we have learned what competition may accomplish. Even Marx admits that it has been much. Quite apart from communism or any other system, is there need for all of these countries and the whole world to learn of the possibilities of cooperation? If so, Russia may prove the world's laboratory in cooperative and industrialized farming.

The socialization of all life may prove a major experiment in this great laboratory of life. From the beginnings of mutual aid in animal life, from the early groupings of men in family, tribe, city, state or nation, in ever-widening circles of growing unity, men seem to be marching on, often unconsciously, in an "Open Conspiracy" toward an integrated, organized, cooperative world of peace and creative construction. And this, despite the backward eddies of conflict, war and strife. Almost every advance of modern civilization has been a social achievement. But who has discovered even the distant approaches to the possibilities of socialized government, industry or agriculture; of socialized education, culture, or art; of socialized medicine, law, recreation or human welfare? Must not all of life be both individualized and socialized, for the one and the many, for the potential personality and the great society? If so, may not the socialism of Russia and the individual liberalism of America both be vast laboratories of social experiment? Is it possible that, overlooking the individual limitations of each, as a type Henry Ford and Karl Marx may both have a contribution to make to humanity? If so, why should we despise either, or look with dread upon anything merely because it is new? Has Mr. Ford alone, or his type, solved as yet the problems of unemployment, poverty, or slums? If not, why not look to the human laboratory for possible solutions both in individual and social life?

It must be remembered that time is a factor in this long-distance race of the Russian experiment. A foreign press has been too obviously eager not only to exaggerate but to gloat over the misfortunes of Soviet Russia. It is unfair to compare the United States, with the full development of her vast resources a century and a half after her Revolution, with Russia, less than a decade out of almost chaos and poverty. Russia must be given time. The French

Revolution of 1789 could destroy the rotten Bourbon government, but it was long replaced by the guillotine and anarchy, the despotism of Napoleon, and the return of the Bourbons in counter-revolution. Not until 1870, eighty years after the Revolution, was a really permanent democratic republic established. The long hostility of monarchist Europe to revolutionary France finds its parallel in the attitude toward Soviet Russia today. If there is any philosophy of history there should be lessons to learn from revolutionary France, remembering that the republics of the United States, France and Soviet Russia were all born of revolution.

Emil Ludwig suggestively compares and contrasts the French and Russian Revolutions.[1] Both in 1789 and 1917 masses were motivated by a burning passion for social justice. In both the action was national but the idea was international, for the French Revolution was in intention a world revolution and ultimately affected the whole world. Almost all the civil liberties of Europe had their origin in that movement, while "similar indirect effects of the Russian movement are making themselves felt." The clericals and nobles who were in complete control of Bourbon France were estimated by Sieyès at 200,000. This was just the number of the landlords who owned over a quarter of the arable land in European Czarist Russia. King Louis and the neurotic Czar Nicholas, alike in their weakness, were both dethroned, imprisoned and put to death. The Reign of Terror under Danton and Robespierre lasted about two

[1] *Nineteenth Century,* October, 1930, p. 459.

years. It became ever more radical and passed from the demand for political to economic equality: "There must be neither rich nor poor." The French revolutionary court was similar to the Cheka. Both countries had to contend with foreign intervention bent on overthrowing the revolution. Lenin modified his program by the New Economic Policy in the sixth year, as the French Revolution did in the fifth year after the storming of the Bastile. But whereas in the twelfth year the extremes of the French Revolution had wellnigh "come to an end," in the twelfth year Stalin had begun to intensify and reassert the full program of the Soviet Revolution.

The atheistic movement in the French Revolution was at the beginning fiercer than the Russian. Both countries abolished the old calendar. Both made every fifth day a day of rest. The French Convention violently attacked the idea of God and the Church. The beautiful Mme. Mamaros was installed in Notre Dame as the Goddess of Reason. Both movements exhibited caricatures and had processions of protest against the superstitions of religion and the corruptions of the Church. In the seventh year after the French Revolution God was again acknowledged; but it will probably be long before a more tolerant attitude to religion and a radical change of policy will prevail in Russia. However, if history repeats itself, tyranny has never been able indefinitely to maintain itself, and whenever intolerance gives place to tolerance and control to freedom, religion will no doubt reassert itself in Russia as it has in every other land.

CHAPTER XII

RECOGNITION OR NON-RECOGNITION

Based upon the evidence already presented of present conditions in Russia, and the foregoing appraisal both of the merits and demerits of the soviet regime, there would be an honest difference of opinion as to the attitude which the Government of the United States should take toward Russia, and the question of the recognition or non-recognition of its government. In the light of this uncertainty we shall attempt to review the situation.

The tradition of friendship between the United States and Czarist Russia was maintained in spite of the fact that Russia was the last of the great powers to recognize the young American Republic, just as a century and a half later the United States will probably prove to be the last government to recognize Soviet Russia.[1] The United States was the first formally to recognize the new Russian Republic under the provisional government and made them a large loan. President Wilson expressed his sympathy with "the great generous Russian people . . . fighting for freedom." [2] In the sixth of his fourteen points he advocates for Russia "the independent determination of her own

---

[1] In 1809, 33 years after the Declaration of Independence, Russia recognized the United States and John Quincy Adams was sent as the first representative to St. Petersburg. See *American Policy Toward Russia Since 1917*, by Frederick Lewis Schuman, University of Chicago, International Publishers, p. 14. We are indebted to this admirable volume in this section.

[2] Ibid, p. 34.

political development," adding, "the treatment accorded to Russia by her sister nations in the months to come will be the acid test of their good will, of their comprehension of her needs as distinguished from their own interests, and of their intelligent and unselfish sympathy." [1]

In the period of divided authority between the waning influence of Kerensky and the growing power of the Soviets, Ambassador Francis consistently favored the former and opposed the soviet regime. Under his advice America began, as it were, "to put her money on the wrong horse," at least on the losing horse. Francis advised the execution of Lenin and Trotzky for treason, as paid German agents. [2] Raymond Robins, on the other hand, who became head of the American Red Cross Mission, advocated cooperation with the growing Soviet power. On March 5, 1918, Trotzky made to him a memorable proposal that the Soviet Government would defeat the ratification of the Brest-Litovsk treaty and resume the war against the Central Powers if America and the Allies would aid Russia in her struggle against Germany. [3] The acceptance of that offer would have greatly changed the whole subsequent course of events. But when no reply came from Washington, Russia was forced to ratify the humiliating Brest-Litovsk treaty.

---

[1] Ibid, p. 71. *Russian American Relations*, p. 74.

[2] Ibid, p. 50. See David R. Francis, *Russia from the American Embassy*, pp. 24–25. Kerensky fled in the car of the secretary of the American Embassy. Francis refers to the new cabinet headed by Lenin as "disgusting." He addressed a message to the people of Russia warning them that "a desperate foe is sowing the seeds of dissension in your midst." Ibid, pp. 55–59.

[3] *Russian American Relations*, pp. 81–82.

Ambassador Francis advocated intervention against the Soviet Government.[1] Lenin entrusted to Robins an elaborate plan of Russian-American commercial relations, which on July 1, 1918, Robins presented to the State Department in Washington, pointing out the madness of forcible Allied military intervention against the will of the Russian people, but he was unable even to secure an interview with President Wilson. The President was long opposed to armed intervention but finally yielded to Francis' fatal appeal for a policy which finally developed into armed intervention and a war to overthrow the Soviet Republic.[2] Russia was invaded, blockaded, and disrupted with subsidized civil war, American money and lives were sacrificed, and thousands suffered death in Russia, while at one time the Soviet Government was fighting upon a dozen fronts.

There was no formal declaration by either side but a war of almost unparalleled ferocity developed. White Russians as well as Red inaugurated a reign of terror. Finally in disgust the Czechoslovaks, on whose behalf intervention had been undertaken, protested with the Americans against "criminal actions that will stagger the entire world; the burning of villages, the murder of masses of peaceful in-

[1] *Schuman,* p. 89; *Francis,* pp. 297–301.

[2] President Wilson, dreading intervention, probably felt that American participation rather than abstention would enable her to mitigate its evils and determine its purposes. The Allied force in the North about Archangel consisted of 6,000 British, 4,500 Americans, 1,500 Frenchmen, with contingents of White Russians and other nationalities. General Graves commanded the American Expeditionary Force of 7,000 in Siberia, which refrained from fighting as far as possible. Japan seized the opportunity to rush in 70,000 men. The Expedition cost the United States, $3,000,000, 244 soldiers killed and 305 wounded. *Schuman,* p. 137.

habitants, and the shooting of hundreds of persons of democratic convictions." [1]   Red terror and White seemed to vie
with the Allies who "felt obliged to arrest and execute sus-
pects on a wholesale scale." [2]   Intervention, counter-revolution and atrocities united the majority of the Russian people
against the foreign invaders.   The Red armies, victorious
on all fronts, were finally able to drive out the last foreign
invader and subdue the last of the White armies. [3]

More effective and more fatal than armed intervention
was the American and Allied propaganda against Russia.
Long silent about the White Terror, even the *New York
Times* pictured Russia as a "Gigantic Bedlam," where
"Maniacs Stalked Raving Through the Streets." [4]   Char-
acteristic of the propaganda was the fabrication about the
"nationalization of women" which was attributed to the
Soviets based upon a false decree attributed to the local
Association of Anarchists in Saratov on March 15, 1918. [5]
It had never been either proposed or practiced by the com-

[1] Czechoslovak Memorandum to Allied Representatives at Vladivostok,
Nov. 15, 1919. *Schuman,* p. 118.

[2] Ibid, p. 138.

[3] Foreign Minister Chicherin addressed a note to President Wilson on
October 24: "Mr. President, the 'acid test' of the relations between the
United States and Russia gave quite different results from those that
might have been expected from your message to Congress. But we have
reason not to be altogether dissatisfied with even these results, since the
outrages of the counter-revolution in the East and North have shown the
workers and peasants of Russia the aims of the Russian counter-revolution, and of its foreign supporters, thereby creating among the Russian
people an iron will to defend their liberty and the conquests of the revolution." Ibid, p. 121. *Russian American Relations,* pp. 258–266.

[4] March 11, 1919, 1:5.

[5] *Schuman,* pp. 123, 153. See *Congressional Record,* Vol. 57, Part 5,
pp. 4882–88; and 1388–1395; pp. 1970–74.

munists. The State Department announced: "The rumor as to the nationalization of women is untrue." *New Europe* admitted its mistake with an apology for publishing the report. Yet even *Current History* still tried to maintain the story by descriptions of "eye witnesses." Such false propaganda widely circulated, and never to this day contradicted by much of the American press, has contrived to keep up a feeling of fear and hostility which cannot now easily be removed. Senator Borah and others long protested in vain against intervention and later consistently advocated recognition of the Russian Republic.[1]

Herbert Hoover, as Director of the American Relief Administration, during the famine, conducted the humane and highly efficient relief of distress which was so gratefully appreciated by the Russian people.[2] He favored the lifting of the blockade against Russia in order to reveal the complete "foolishness" of the soviet industrial system to the Russian people.[3] As Secretary of Commerce, he declared: "Under their economic system, no matter how much they moderate it in name, there can be no real return to production in Russia, and therefore Russia will have no consider-

---

[1] On September 5, 1918, Senator Borah said: "While we are not at war with Russia, while Congress has not declared war, we are carrying on war with the Russian people. . . . Whatever is done in that country in the way of armed intervention is without constitutional authority . . . or plain usurpation of power to maintain troops in Russia at this time." 378 *Congressional Record,* vol. 58, Part 5, pp. 4896–98.

[2] The A. R. A. had collected $66,300,000, shipped 912,121 tons of food, and with a staff of 200 Americans and 80,000 Russians had saved from death by starvation some ten million people. Schuman, p. 206, *A. R. A. Annual Report,* 1923, p. 12.

[3] Committee For the Regeneration of Russia, *The Blockade of Soviet Russia,* p. 26.

able commodities to export, and consequently no great ability to obtain imports . . . That requires the abandonment of their present economic system." [1]

President Harding maintained the American policy of non-recognition, after other countries had recognized the Soviet Republic, upon the grounds of protest against "a policy of confiscation and repudiation." [2]

President Coolidge, however, in his first message to Congress, on December 6, 1923, suggested a possible change of policy and recognition based upon the three conditions of compensation for confiscation of the property of American citizens, recognition of the American debt, and abatement of the spirit of enmity to our institutions.[3] Ten days later Foreign Minister Chicherin addressed a cablegram to President Coolidge informing him of the complete readiness of the Soviet Government "to discuss with your Government all problems mentioned in your message, these negotiations being based upon the principle of mutual non-intervention in internal affairs." [4]

---

[1] *Schuman,* p. 201. *New York Times,* March 22, 1921, 1:2.

[2] July 31, 1923, *New York Times,* August 1, 1923. This was in his last address, undelivered because of illness, at the full height of the activity of the "Ohio gang."

[3] President Coolidge said: "We have every desire to see that great people, who are our traditional friends, restored to their position among the nations of the earth. . . . Whenever there appears any disposition to compensate our citizens who were despoiled and to recognize that debts contracted with our government, not by the Czar, but by the newly formed Republic of Russia; whenever the active spirit of enmity to our institutions is abated; whenever there appear works meet for repentance, our country ought to be the first to go to the economic and moral rescue of Russia." *Congressional Record,* Vol. 65, p. 451, Dec. 20, 1923.

[4] Chicherin cabled: "After reading your message to Congress, the Soviet Government, sincerely anxious to establish at last firm friendship

Immediately, however, Secretary Hughes replied with a curt message declining all conference and negotiations and declaring that the American Government had incurred no liabilities to Russia.[1] By 1926 twenty-two states had recognized the Soviet Government, including Great Britain, France, Germany, Italy, Japan and all the principal nations except the United States, which still remained obdurate. Russia's war and pre-war debts totalled over six billion dollars.[2] Of this the debt to America, with interest, may

---

[1] Secretary Hughes thus replied to the Chicherin communication, on December 18, 1923:

"There would seem to be at this time no reason for negotiations. The American Government . . . is not proposing to barter away its principles.

"If the Soviet authorities are ready to restore the confiscated property of American citizens or make effective compensation they can do so.

"If the Soviet authorities are ready to repeal their decree repudiating Russia's obligations to this country and appropriately recognize them, they can do so.

"It requires no conference or negotiations to accomplish these results, which can and should be achieved at Moscow as evidence of good faith.

"The American Government has not incurred liabilities to Russia or repudiated obligations.

"Most serious is the continued propaganda to overthrow the institutions of this country. This Government can enter into no negotiations until these efforts directed from Moscow are abandoned." *Congressional Record*, Vol. 65, p. 451, December 20, 1923.

[2] Of Russia's pre-war government debt France holds 80 per cent and Great Britain 14 per cent. The war debt is owed to Great Britain, 70 per cent, to France 19 per cent, and to the United States 7 per cent. Russia's

---

with the people and Government of the United States, informs you of its complete readiness to discuss with your government all problems mentioned in your message, these negotiations being based on the principle of mutual non-intervention in internal affairs. The Soviet Government will continue whole-heartedly to adhere to this principle, expecting the same attitude from the American Government. As to the question of claims mentioned in your message, the Soviet Government is fully prepared to negotiate with a view toward its satisfactory settlement on the assumption that the principle of reciprocity will be recognized all around."

be reckoned at about $276,500,000. The claims of American citizens and private companies against Soviet Russia represent approximately $300,000,000.[1]

The Soviet Republic, like the revolutionary French Republic before it, repudiated state debts of the old monarchy,[2] and brought forward counter-claims of damages for the Allied intervention and blockade. It must be remembered that Allied intervention in Siberia was undertaken at the express invitation of the United States and that intervention is an illegal act, which in case of its failure, renders the state liable to claims for damages.[3] Intervention in Russia was continued for fifteen months after the armistice. Professor Schuman of the University of Chicago writes: "We thus reach the conclusion that Allied and American intervention in Russia cannot be justified under any of the

---

[1] Principal and Interest of Debt to U. S. Government
(Moulton) $276,500,000
Debts Privately held in U. S. A. 86,000,000
Confiscation and Destruction of Property of American
Nationals 300,000,000

$662,500,000

Schuman, p. 301; Moulton, p. 181.

[2] Decree of January 21 and February 8, 1918. Schuman, p. 73.
[3] Schuman, pp. 304–305.

---

war debt to Great Britain is reckoned by Moulton at $2,687,000,000; to France $746,000,000, to the United States approximately $276,500,000. Chicherin at Geneva claimed some $6,106,580,000 for direct damages during the intervention and civil war. *Russian Debts* by Pasvolsky and Moulton, pp. 21, 22, 181. See *American Policy Toward Russia,* pp. 298, 310.

accepted principles of international law."[1] Certainly American forces in Murmansk, Archangel, and Siberia did damage to Russian property and were responsible for the loss of Russian lives. This intervention was not undertaken for national defence, and was without a declaration of war. Its illegality would probably be upheld in any impartial court of international law.

Of the three conditions laid down by President Coolidge the first two financial conditions are not insurmountable. The claims of American firms are not large and could doubtless be settled. The American debt is also relatively small and could probably be adjusted.[2] Responsibility for unwillingness even to confer concerning these conditions must rest with the United States.

It is the third condition, concerning propaganda and hostility, that is much more crucial. There is probably evidence to show that the Soviet Government itself would refrain from any propaganda or interference in the internal affairs of the United States. If Americans refused to credit them with sincerity Russia could easily reply by

---

[1] *American Policy Toward Russia*, p. 309.

Professor Schuman says: "It was an ill-considered act of policy, wholly without justification in law, the failure of which subjects the governments involved to full responsibility for compensating the aggrieved party for the losses suffered from it. The Russian counter-claims appear in principles to be quite proper." Pasvolsky and Moulton declare that "even if Russia should honor her existing debts, she cannot pay them." *Russian Debts,* p. 155.

[2] In October, 1926, Krassin, Soviet envoy in London, stated that his government was prepared to drop counter-claims and acknowledge its debt to the United States in full, if negotiations were opened, but the Russian attitude is much more independent today. Schuman, p. 314. *Washington Evening Star,* Oct. 9, 1926.

asking whether the United States had ever effectively interfered in the internal affairs of other nations, to make or unmake governments in Latin America, as in Mexico, Nicaragua, Costa Rica, etc. However genuine the neutrality of the Soviet Government might be, there is no denial that the Russian Communist Party largely influences and at times almost directs both the Soviet Government and the Communist International. There is no question whatever that the policy of this Third International is one of world revolution. It has been, it is, and it will continue to be such, with or without recognition. This has never been denied in Russia.

The question is, however, whether the hostility of the Soviet Government and the activities of the Third International would be increased or diminished by recognition. All things considered, twenty-four other governments, not one of which agree with the policies of communism, have thought it on the whole the part of wisdom to recognize the Soviet Government.

There are strong arguments that can be advanced by equally sincere men both for and against recognition. A fair consideration of some of the reasons for the recognition of the present Russian government might include the following:

1. According to the prevailing foreign policy of the United States, recognition, on the *de facto* theory, does not imply approval of policy but simply the ability of a government effectively to control the state. After the French Revolution England and most of monarchical Europe refused to recognize the Republic of France. Washington

agreed with Jefferson in declaring it to be the American policy "to acknowledge any government to be rightful which is formed by the will of the nation, substantially declared." [1] Despite the regicide, the guillotine and the red terror, although approving of none of these things, the United States recognized the French Republic in 1793.   We had recognized the Czarist government despite its centuries of tyranny and terror.   We had recognized the government of Turkey in spite of the massacres of Abdul Hamid.   Recognition did not imply approval of policy.

When Germany emerged from the war red-handed from the chopping off of children's hands and endless barbarities, according to Allied propaganda since proved largely false, was it the part of wisdom to "hang the Kaiser and make Germany pay," driving her as an outlaw into alliance with Russia, Japan and her late allies?   Or was it better to seek to bring her into the League of Nations, and enter into treaties that might lead to peace and prosperity?

It was not primarily a question of what Germany deserved, or whether Allied propaganda was true or false, but of what was best for all the nations concerned. . When Britain and France recognized Soviet Russia they did not approve of her system nor of her propaganda but they felt better able to cope with it when she was bound by agreements and under close official observation than when the movement was outlawed and driven under ground.   After

---

[1] Schuman, p. 267.   The same view was followed in the recognition of the new states of Latin America in their revolt from Spain and prevailingly until Woodrow Wilson's refusal to recognize Huerta in Mexico.

giving a hearing to communist soap-box orators in Hyde Park, the crowd heckles them, laughs at them and goes home in good humor.   The British believe that they are far safer thus than under a witch-hunting, heresy-hunting regime of fear, that sees an imaginary bolshevik under every chair, and has no faith in its own institutions.   The United States has negotiated in every other case involving war debts and confiscation.   Why are we unwilling even to negotiate with a country that every other great nation has recognized? If we have recognized despots, dictatorships, slave states, polygamists; if we have dealt with cannibals and red-handed revolutionists, why can we not treat with Russia which has a stable government and is stronger today than it was thirteen years ago?

2. The failure of our past policy of intervention and non-recognition, when compared to the plan of recognition followed by the other great nations, would not seem to be satisfactory.   What have we accomplished by non-recognition?   Can we isolate one-sixth of the world that is in closer contact with Asia than are the nations of the West? Can we abolish the Communist International or prevent its activities by refusing recognition?   Can we overthrow the present regime in Russia by force or by invasion?   If, combined with the Allies and all the White Russians, when the country was in poverty and chaos, we could not conquer Russia in the hour of her greatest weakness, what can we do by force in the time of her strength?   As Napoleon found in 1812, it would be quite impossible to conquer any vast

territory like Russia, Canada or the United States by an invading force.

Have we no faith in our own form of government and its institutions and privileges that we think a handful of communists could so easily overthrow it?[1] Why should the American working man, with his high wages, his automobile, his home, his liberty, his many privileges, wish to exchange them for the poverty, the hardships and the dictatorship of Russia? If we are afraid of unemployment, surely we are rich enough to do for our unemployed what a score of advanced industrial nations have done, and set our own house in order without any thought or fear of bolshevism.

Although such a counsel of despair gains during a period of unemployment, the decline of communism in America during the last decade is shown by the membership rolls of the party factions. More than a decade ago they claimed a handful of some 40,000. Today there are less than 15,000. The communist leader, Jay Lovestone, admitted that the membership had fallen to 6,145 at the beginning of 1930. The movement is almost microscopic and relatively impotent in America and England. If we recognized Russia, the moment a communist infringes our statutes we have ready our courts, prisons and deportation orders. If a diplomat

---

[1] Roy W. Howard, President of the Scripps-Howard Newspaper Service, wrote to Reeve Schley, vice-president of the Chase National Bank: "Personally I think the menace of Bolshevism in the United States is about as great as the menace of sunstroke in Greenland or chilblains in the Sahara." *The Soviets in World Affairs,* by Louis Fischer, p. 560.

abused his privileges we could demand his immediate recall as has been done at other times.

3. A new situation both in Russia and in the United States suggests the desirability of closer trade relations. Whatever may be said of the past, when its fall was eagerly prophesied every few weeks, the present government in Russia is more stable than it has ever been. It is probably one of the most stable governments in Europe today. However much we may dislike it, as we have seen it has probably come to stay—at least for a very long time. If it has come to stay we must in time trade with Russia. The only question is, shall it be upon favorable or unfavorable terms?

Have we reason to fear their economic recovery? A prosperous Russia will be a good customer. For decades to come she will need our products. But it is quite certain that she can and will reduce her trade with the United States and buy every possible commodity from others if we continue our attitude of latent hostility. As the foreign office stated in Moscow to our American party: "If you do not change your present policy, we shall certainly change ours."

Russia has a strange liking for America and American methods. She looks with admiration on the industrial efficiency of Henry Ford, the General Electric Company and the International Harvester. She has already had large and profitable dealings with all of them and would like to extend her trade with us. Nearly a thousand American engineers, experts and technicians are now employed in Russia, most of them more highly paid than they would be in any country in the world. Russia has on the whole scrupulously fulfilled her trade agreements. After the Wall Street panic of October, 1929, faced by a possible buyers' strike in Europe, Russia alone voluntarily increased her purchases and became for a time one of the six largest buyers from the United States.[1]

The S. S. Europa, on her maiden voyage, brought Russian technicians and $30,000,000 worth of orders for American machinery. Yet our trade with Russia today is only a fraction of what it might be. Without consuls or trade representatives, without contacts or adequate arrangements for credit, it is heavily handicapped. Even so it has reached the value of over $150,000,000 a year. Russia's foreign trade, already nearly worth a billion dollars, is to be doubled in the next four years, according to plans that are usually carried out. But she can divert her purchases into the most favored channels. Her trade has been usually sensitive to political relations. The fruitless Arcos raid by the London police was followed by a sharp decline of British imports and an immediate increase of American and German trade. Recent recognition of the Soviet Government by Great Britain and new trade agreements brought an early order of nearly $15,000,000 for the firm of Imperial Chemicals and the prospect of $100,000,000 a year increase for British exports. It is quite possible that many foreign business men who want to capture Russia's trade would do all in their power to persuade the United States not to recognize Russia. But recognition, with the increased confidence it would in-

---

[1] *Current History*, September, 1930, p. 1069.

spire, contacts and credit that would follow, would very materially affect America's trade with Russia.

4. World peace would probably be affected even more than prosperity by recognition. Many believe that we should have friendly, direct and official relations with every government which has signed the Kellogg Pact. Non-recognition inevitably carries the implication of latent hostility. Russia keenly feels this. Our genuineness in offering the Kellogg Pact would imply the elimination of suspicion and the institution of all possible direct channels for the solution of all disputes. But the first and most obvious of these would be normal diplomatic intercourse.

There can be no effective world-wide reduction of armaments that leaves Russia out. Europe cannot proportionately disarm while ignoring Russia. Russia, like Germany, has a vital interest in disarmament. When she proposed to the League of Nations Disarmament Commission first complete disarmament, and then, failing that, a fifty per cent reduction, there is evidence to show that she was genuine though, like Germany, not disinterested. Her neighbors of Poland, Roumania, and the Little Entente backed by France all have proportionately larger armies than Russia.

Russia is convinced that she is to be invaded by some of these western powers. There is a manifest fear psychosis and a consequent defensive militarism that is very evident and widespread in Russia today. This is behind the difficulty over the Chinese Eastern Railway and their haste to speed up the five year plan. Because of this fear complex those who dissent from or oppose the government's economic program, especially if backed by the religious elements within Russia or the protests of religious bodies without, are being treated with a severity that is usual only for conscientious objectors in wartime. This persecution increases when the government believes it is menaced from without. It is the conviction of the writer and of many observers in Russia today that this war fear, together with economic and religious persecution, would be greatly lessened if Russia were drawn into friendly intercourse with the rest of the world. Russia undoubtedly is endeavoring to build a new social order that will differ radically from that of other nations and that is bound to challenge the old order at many points. There are serious evils in this Soviet system which many of the friends of Russia earnestly desire to see lessened or changed. Can that best be done by war or peace?

It is idle to say that we shall be neutral. We could not maintain our neutrality in the world war, and we cannot do so toward Russia. We must either recognize a stable government in Russia and establish friendly trade relations with her, or else treat her as an outcast, a moral leper, in cold and implacable latent hostility.

As in the case of Germany, it is not now primarily a question of what Russia deserves from our point of view, but what is best for the peace and prosperity of the world. Some nations have tried intervention, invasion, false propaganda, a hunger blockade, a world boycott, ceaseless latent hostility. And with what result? Has not the time arrived when, as in the case of our late enemy Germany, we should try the method of friendship, recognition and maximum trade?

CHAPTER XIII

THE OUTLOOK FOR THE FUTURE

Dr. Nicholas Murray Butler states that the world has come to one of those great turning points when humanity is once more being compelled to reconsider the question which from the beginning of history constituted the very heart of the problem of political and social progress—the question of the rights of the one and of the many. Neither an extreme individualism nor a rigid collectivism seems to offer a panacea. He claims that only a liberalism that secures the rights of all can check communism. Conversely only a communism that in the end dares to restore the liberties of all can meet liberalism.

The advantages and disadvantages, the gains and losses both of capitalism and communism stand out in contrast as one compares the two systems. On the one hand there are the obvious advantages of a capitalistic system that is automatic, that develops initiative and invention, permits a maximum of freedom, favors efficiency and the lower costs of mass production, and can point to such a measure of material success, higher wages and a higher standard of living. On the other hand, one must debit the obvious wastes of capitalism, the business cycle of overproduction, depression and periodic unemployment, the competition and duplication in production and distribution, the high cost of advertising and competitive salesmanship, the over-expansion, lack of coordination, the waste of luxury production, the exhaustion of natural resources, the early scrapping of wage earners, the lack of planning for the future, vast inequalities and injustices with their resultant class antagonism and ill-will, the neglect of the human factor, and the sacrifice or prostitution of almost everything in the system to the individual profit of a small minority.

Communism dares to affirm high social ideals and stakes its faith in human nature upon them. It appeals to higher incentives than the profit motive. It maintains the simple life for all, and consequently an all-important and essential equality. It refuses to measure success in terms of money or personal prestige, but tests every result, every law, every achievement according to its social value. It cares for the poor and favors the long-neglected masses and the majority.

There are obvious advantages in a vast coordination of all economic activity in a plan of the whole for national and international life. There are gains in even an approximately classless society. There are limitless potentialities in the further development of cooperation, in the release of energies when the whole mass of labor is given fuller opportunity for personal, social and political development. There may be hitherto undreamed of possibilities in the socialization of agriculture, in relating industry so closely to government, to the producing workers and the consuming public, in drawing education from the very heart of life and relating it to every practical and vital issue; in submitting the government to the vigilant and constant review of the workers in town and country; in placing every part of life in the crucible of criticism and submitting it to the scientific laboratory tests of ever-fresh creative experience.

There are advantages in the absence of stoppages and strikes which, though permitted, are brief and infrequent; in the winning of labor from opposition to positive constructive effort in increasing output and improving production; in harnessing the herd feelings of workers' control and the dynamic of class consciousness to efficient management and to national and world welfare, instead of being negatively ranged on the side of protest and obstruction.   There is a gain in the elimination of former luxury production and the reduction of non-productive occupations and persons and the concentration of the national energies upon social welfare. There are creative possibilities in any system that can inspire a new spirit of collective unity based on the fundamental, democratic equality of "a control of the workers by workers in the interests of the workers and not by and for a superior class." [1]   A new spirit of creation, of expression, of release of long-repressed or unsuspected forces is abroad in this "laboratory of life."   According to the records of the Central Bureau of Workers' Inventions, whereas before the revolution an average of 4000 applications a year were received for inventions, since the revolution it has risen to over 12,000 and shows a constant tendency to increase.

---

[1] *Russian Economic Development Since the Revolution* by Maurice Dobb of Cambridge, England, p. 382–388. We are indebted to Mr. Dobb in his appraisal of the relative advantages and disadvantages of the two systems.

Worker and peasant now hold their heads up. The country is theirs and they know it. There is a spirit of adventure and of indomitable achievement in the air. They feel that this workers' state is something new, and it does not yet appear what it shall be.

But as Trotzky on the one hand and Norman Angel on the other point out, each system must be judged by its fruits. Which system will in the end produce more, cheaper and better goods? Which will eventuate in greater human welfare? Theoretically a functional society ought to be superior to an acquisitive one. But will it prove so in practice? The answer cannot be settled by the dogmatism of vehement propaganda on either side, nor will it be decided in a decade. It would have been unfair to judge of the possibilities of the North American Republic ten years after Valley Forge. The United States has had over a century and a half to develop its economic system and its resources since 1776; Russia has had not a decade and a half since 1917.

Thus far, however, there are certain defects and disadvantages in the Russian system which may or may not be overcome. The efficiency of management and the lack of competent technicians still leaves much to be desired. The red tape of the administrative system and its wooden inflexibility are still painful. A highly centralized administrative control is burdened with unessential details, while the demand for endless statistics, studies and commissions divert management from its proper function.[1] If Henry Ford

---

[1] Rykov quotes one manager as complaining of nine separate control commissions and inspections of his works: "My time is wasted in a

dared not act without consulting a committee and could not
trust his subordinates with large responsibility what contribution could he have made to industry? The burden of
officialdom, the sheer loss of time occasioned by cumbersome
administrative machinery, the inability or fear of assuming
large responsibility for immediate decision and bold action
when there is an ubiquitous, invisible and incalculable political police to be reckoned with, are severe handicaps.
Although social solidarity has its undiscovered possibilities
to develop, individual worth, initiative, personal freedom
and liberty of conscience, with their hard-won bill of rights
and Magna Carta of liberty achieved more than seven centuries ago, may not be brushed aside by a contemptuous
gesture, and will have to be provided for in any system
which is to endure in the future or challenge the allegiance
of free men. If with Hegel and Croce it is maintained that
the chief lesson of history is freedom, that its whole development may be interpreted as the unfolding idea of liberty, no
"temporary" dictatorships, however natural or excusable, no
backward moving eddies in the main current of human
progress, can be mistaken for its main trend. Probably no
permanent denial of liberty will effectively appeal to hu-

---

most unproductive manner on reports, conferences, negotiations, etc.
. . . When am I to find time for work?" This manager was later sum-
moned before the political police on "a childish whim" of the G. P. U.
Rykov concludes: "Our system of economic administration even today
is still centralized to a degree based on mistrust of every minor link of
the chain." This mistrust has later been shown not only of "minor
links" but of many leaders of commanding ability like Rykov himself.
See *Russian Economic Development*, p. 387, and the Report of Rykov at
the Fifteenth Party Congress, November, 1926.

manity. It must be remembered, however, that both the systems of capitalism and communism are on trial. They stand over against one another, separated almost in watertight compartments, misunderstanding one another, misrepresenting one another, fearing each other. Each has attributed the basest motives to the actions of the other. Each counts the leaders in the other system, whether capitalist or communist, as dishonest or hypocritical.

Our effort throughout this book has been an attempt to understand Russia. This is difficult at best but it should not be impossible. We have spoken of the significance of Russia, where the largest country in the world is trying the boldest social experiment in history, endeavoring to build an entirely new social order based upon a new philosophy of life, with new motivations, objectives and ideals. It is not only a new order parallel to ours but challenging our own at every point.

We examined communism in theory and practice and endeavored to trace the phases of its development. We then considered the new experiment in collective agriculture and the effort to industrialize urban and rural Russia by the daring but costly five year plan entailing such hardship for the workers. We next examined the structure and organization of the Communist Party, which seeks to combine wide democratic discussion and participation by the organized workers and peasants, with efficient but dangerous centralization of power in the hands of a small group, rigorously excluding or crushing any deviation to the left or right of their policies and program. We saw how this group largely controls the Communist Party and through it both the Government of Soviet Russia and the Comintern, or Third International. The latter controls in turn communist individuals and groups in every nation throughout the world. Here is a movement of unique solidarity and uniformity throughout the world.

We briefly examined soviet culture and its system of education, frankly designed as propaganda to train the rising generation of Russia for effective leadership in a world movement. We then examined their new moral standards, their conception of marriage and the home, and their powerful youth movement. We tried to understand their attitude toward religion and their practices regarding it.

We sought to evaluate the serious evils that seemed to be not merely accidental and temporary but inherent in the very essence of the system as a logical and unescapable part of its present phase. These evils include a dictatorship that tends to take the form at times of a tyranny and even of a terror, and which, instead of being "temporary," has a tendency not only to perpetuate itself indefinitely but to become ever more intense; secondly the principle and strategy not only of world revolution as a panacea for all social ills, but of a continuing revolution that ends only when the last bourgeois enemy ceases to exist; and thirdly the harsh and intolerant dogmatism of the system that manifests itself in the suppression of divergent free thought, speech or action, and at times in the persecution of religion as among the sectarians in Russia today.

We then considered the challenge of communism, despite these evils, in its passion for social justice and sharing with the poor; its aim of a classless society free from all prejudice of race, color or nationality; its provision of a kind of world laboratory of social experiment.

After evaluating its merits and demerits we advocated the recognition of Soviet Russia as a *de facto* government, not on the ground of its merits but for the sake of the prosperity and peace of the world. We believe that neither recognition nor non-recognition will end the propaganda of communists in America, but that this can best be dealt with, not by the ruthless savagery of police clubs, but by putting our own house in order, by giving social justice to our workers and then dealing firmly with lawbreakers by our own courts, thoroughly cleansed and reformed.

We find ourselves at the end, as in the beginning, with two conflicting social orders confronting one another—capitalism and communism. A loosely organized or disorganized liberalism has developed individual initiative with its amazing accomplishments under competitive industrialism, nationalism, imperialism and militarism. But something seems to be at fault. One reason why many of us hate communism is because of a troubled conscience. Our vast social wrongs stare us in the face and will not down. There are the evils of our unjust distribution of wealth and income; wealth irresponsible and unshared side by side with poverty unrelieved. There are shameful slums carelessly accepted almost as a matter of course, after a city like Vienna has practically ended this abomination forever. Child labor continues after defeating two federal amendments to our Constitution which sought to abolish it, increasing in many states after it has been forbidden in Russian industry. For years there has been criminally neglected unemployment, met only by wasteful and inefficient spasms of public works, inadequate temporary relief and "charity" long after a score of the most advanced industrial nations have given the worker justice in a legitimate self-respecting system of unemployment insurance to which the employee regularly contributes as he does to his life insurance.

The present organization of society is the cause of a whole brood of social evils. America has an income in normal times sufficient to insure a comfortable living for all. This amounted to $3,745 for a family of five in 1928. Poverty and protracted involuntary unemployment in the United States are chiefly due to mal-distribution of the national income. The cream is first skimmed off by the larger fortunes. The 15,780 persons with incomes over $100,000 had an aggregate income of $4,903,000,000. The 936,470 persons with incomes over $5000 received a total income of nearly nineteen billion dollars. Two billion dollars a year from unearned income would end most serious unemployment and provide a fund for legitimate insurance, to which the workers could also contribute. Leading foreign nations tax large unearned incomes from two to four times as heavily as does the United States.

After deducting the above nineteen billion dollars from the national income, it left for the 23,100,000 families with incomes under $5000, only some $65,340,000,000 of which they can spend a maximum of only about $37,830,000,000 for the $55,000,000,000 value of our manufactures, excluding exports. Through mal-distribution we suffer at once from over-production and under-consumption. While there is an over-production of wheat at prices fatal to the American and Canadian farmer, yet millions are hungry. While there is an over-production of cotton and wool, millions shiver without sufficient clothing. Long bread lines of unemployed young men haunt our great cities. They starve in the midst of plenty and are left idle because they have produced too much.

We are in the midst of exploitation and chaos due to a planless system. We have harnessed power-driven machinery to the profit motive. We have harnessed a billion and a half horsepower of energy but our machines have run away with us. For uncoordinated, blind profit too many automobile factories, too many flour and textile mills and twice too many coal mines were opened. Over-production and under-consumption result. On an average of about every seven years unplanned production and inequitable distribution result in the cycle of a business crisis or depression.

At the moment of writing, men are not only unemployed in our cities but many of them, hungry and desperate, are being demoralized and broken for life. Seventeen nations, including Great Britain, France, Germany, Italy and Austria, have either compulsory or subsidized systems of unemployment insurance, insuring some 45,000,000 workers. We have nothing better to offer them than a spasm of charity and temporary relief for a few. We have millions for charity but how much have we for planned production for use, instead of production for the private profit of a few? Have we the intelligence and conscience to control the machines we have made in the interest of human welfare for all? Have we no other thought than to hope for a return of "prosperity" to start the cycle all over again of over-production, speculation, depression and under-consumption? Do we see no causal connection between this system of private profiteering and the inevitable parasitic results of economic injustice, crime, lawlessness, racketeering, bootlegging and prostitution—the prostitution of men, women and children to ignorance, incompetence and greed? If these heavy Slavic workingmen and mountaineer peasants like Stalin, who are none too brilliant, have the common sense to insure their few unemployed and then eliminate unemployment altogether, has not America the intelligence and the integrity to remove these injustices and adjust her economic order to human need?

There is our race and color prejudice with its recrudescence of lynching and the apparent determination to "keep the Negro in his place" instead of giving elemental justice before the law, and adequate appropriations for education with full and equal opportunity for an abundant life. If after nineteen centuries of privilege we refuse to admit the Negro to real brotherhood, can we blame the communist or any other system for offering him equal comradeship? Is our civilization to be weighed in the balances and found wanting in these primitive essentials of social justice? If we refuse to permit evolution can we blame oppressed classes for demanding revolution?

The whole competitive system seems to beget strife between classes, nations and races. It leads repeatedly from latent to overt war. The last century alone recorded some forty wars under this system. In the preparatory disarmament commission of the League of Nations in 1930, Russia's Foreign Minister, Maxim Litvinov, who in a previous conference had in vain asked first for complete international disarmament, and failing that, for a fifty per cent reduction in military expenditure, pointed out that since this disarmament commission was established in 1926 the five great powers had, instead of decreasing, actually increased their war budgets by $500,000,000, or 27 per cent annually.

The writer heard Lord Thompson, British Air Minister, just before his death in the crash of the great airship in France, say that Great Britain was spending more than a thousand dollars a minute on preparedness and armament and that America was spending even more than this, or over $800,000,000 a year for the next five years. President Hoover admits that the United States is spending more than any other nation in the world in connection with war, or 72 per cent of the national budget in 1930. The disarmament commission of the League of Nations points out that the world is spending over four billion dollars yearly for war purposes, the burden of which amounts annually to more than $2 per capita or $10 per family for the whole human race.

The "big navy" advocates in the United States are calling for a billion dollar "treaty navy." Meantime the required enrollment of thousands of students in compulsory military training in the R. O. T. C. inculcates the military spirit and makes increasingly difficult the development of the will to peace among many of our youth.

In contrast to the capitalistic system we have offered to us as a panacea, this harsh dictatorship in Russia with its disregard of the rights of the individual, its wanton denial of liberty, the hatred of its class war, its destructive revolution, its scorn for and persecution of some of the finest achievements of our long-struggling humanity. The contemptuous dogmatism of its *ipsi dixit* that communism is the only panacea for the world neither wins the consent of our reason nor overawes us by its threat of force. We at least are not dependent for our daily bread upon the permission of any terror.

As we have seen, two conflicting social orders confront each other. There is already latent warfare between them. Evidences of this are found in fear, in wild rumors, in false propaganda on both sides. Down the streets of Moscow from time to time one sees great red banners warning workers and youth to "Be ready" to repel the coming invasion of Russia by capitalist countries for the overthrow of their sacred revolution and the rights of the workers. Europe and America would think this too childish for words. Their attitude might be, "Who wants to invade Russia in the light of the abysmal failure of former intervention; who dreams of doing so, and who cares whether they have such hysterical fears or not?"

Nevertheless, there is an evident and widespread fear psychosis among the Russian people. It is like petrol ready for the spark. And the leaders in the small group of centralized control, who dominate in one unit all the government, industry, trade, finance, collective agriculture, education, radio broadcasting, film production, platform, public press and police—in a word *all means of communication, information, education and propaganda*—are able to apply the spark to the petrol. They can regulate, control it, even with a perfected silencer and exhaust, and ride upon it as in a powerful and coordinated motor car.

When the Pope made his indignant protests against religious persecution in Russia, this was skilfully turned to account by the leaders of the Soviet Union and one sees today in the Park of Culture and Rest in Moscow, an effigy of the Pope with a death's head under the papal hat, carrying two cannon under his arms, leading a military invasion of Russia. Once again this seems too childish to be taken seriously. But the leaders are able to foment and maintain a kind of continued war psychosis which responds to propaganda with the same heroism, sacrifice and devotion as the millions under arms and in the cities, factories and farms of all the nations of Europe and America responded during the world war, even to the rationing of food, physical privation and dollar-a-year war service. This is a unique and significant phenomenon.

On the other hand, the nations of Europe and America also have a certain fear psychosis concerning Russia. We, too, have our propaganda against them. We are alarmed at the "enormous" dumping of a nation that has less than two per cent of the world's trade. In the morning paper we read, concerning the plan of paving that every tourist sees going on in Moscow, Princess Kropotkin's assurance that the streets are "torn up continually on orders from the government to offer obstacles to street meetings and uprisings against the government."[1] Such a statement is amazing. These "street meetings and uprisings against the government" exist in the imaginations of the princess and of the pathetic White Russian emigrés throughout the world and of apprehensive Americans. Communist meetings of protest in America are sometimes broken up by police clubs, but anti-revolutionary meetings are not allowed in Russia. The workers there, for all their hardships, are better off now than they have ever been and would not take part in such meetings; while others who would count themselves enemies of the regime would not dare to participate. Theoretically, a man might take part in one meeting, but he would never be left at liberty to take part in another, so that as a matter of fact such meetings are not held. Meetings of loud protest, yes, but not uprisings to overthrow the government. It would be as true and as ridiculous to suppose that our American streets are torn up to prevent uprisings. Yet, upon such statements or unwitting propaganda we are continually fed.

----

[1] *New York Times,* November 7. 1930.

In our judgment any system which denies liberty is a
menace, however economically efficient it may be and however great its contributions to social experimentation and
social justice, whether in fascist Italy or communist Russia.
This book looks toward the understanding of Russia,
both as a menace and as a social challenge. It bespeaks an
understanding of both its evil and its good. But how shall
this menace be met? Congressman Fish, with many others
in our country, believes that it can be met by hunting Reds.
If we could break up their meetings and smash their heads
with police clubs, if we could gag them, imprison them like
Mooney and Billings, put them to death like Sacco and
Vanzetti, transport them as in the Palmer raids of our war
hysteria, then we could dwell in peace, they tell us.

But vain is the dream. Our social evils cannot be solved
by a "hush, hush" policy, blind, deaf and dumb to every
social wrong, praying only for a return of "prosperity"
which we can again attribute pharisaically to our superior
virtues. They cannot be solved by a series of "Polly-Anna-
nias" pronouncements telling the rest of the world to pay
their enormous debts, meet our enormous tariffs, and only
to be good that they, as we, may live happily ever afterward.

The solution does not lie either in a return of material
prosperity nor in hunting radicals. The Reds we need mercilessly to hunt are the red wrongs of suffering humanity,
the crying evils of our unjust social order. The only cor-
rective of social wrong is social justice. The remedy for a
planless chaos where social good is an accidental by-product
of competitive profit should be a planned economy of our

own for the whole community. Stuart Chase shows that we can only meet Russia on her own ground by the application of intelligence and organization to our own economic order: "The only final way out lies through planned production . . . If we do not embark on a program of industrial coordination after our own fashion, and that shortly, we shall be driven some day, after God knows what suffering and bloodshed, to the Russian formula. The challenge presented by over-production in an age of a billion horsepower is, to my mind, just as ominous as that." [1]

In the same morning paper in which the Russian princess warns us against Moscow, the Archbishop of Prague, coming nearer home, says: "We live in an era of capitalism, the consequence of which is pauperism. The world's intelligence today is entirely harnessed to the service of capitalism. Great events arise only from a sea of blood. . . . Woe to the nation whose statesmen fail to recognize this. The time is ripe for revolution." [2]

We utterly disagree that great events arise only from a sea of blood. The Archbishop must have been misquoted. Jesus of Nazareth arose from no sea of blood. But no man with a claim to statesmanship should be so blind as merely to warn us concerning the paving torn up in Moscow and of communists in America if he has neither the vision nor courage to seek to right the social wrongs that have driven the long suffering masses of Russia to revolution.

Let us face this issue and not evade it. There is "some-

[1] *Harper's,* November, 1930.
[2] *New York Times,* November 7, 1930, p. 1.

thing rotten" not only in communist Russia, but right here in capitalist America. Do we admit or deny it? Granted that it cannot be lightly changed in a day, do we demand that it shall be changed? Have we or have we not a remedy? If we applied the principles of justice, of mercy, of love, of overcoming evil with good, of the redemption of the evil doer, of peace, instead of war, do we believe that we have the remedy? If so, will we honestly apply it?

If we will not, can we blame others who think that we are too hypocritical or cowardly either to admit these wrongs or to tackle them seriously, for seeking to apply their remedy? If we refuse either to demand or allow social justice by consent, there are those who will seek to impose it by compulsion. The greed of special privilege was blind in Bourbon France, in Hapsburg Austria, in Hohenzollern Prussia, in Czarist Russia. Will it be equally blind in capitalist America? What is disquieting is, not that we have failed as yet patiently to work out a solution, but that we have failed so largely even to see the need of one or to insistently demand it. If any one asks us to put our own house in order, some one cries, "Socialist! Communist! Radical! Pacifist! Traitor!" There is a hysterical, emotional appeal to hunt bolsheviks and silence concerning the evils which they expose.

Hegel, followed by his pupil Marx, maintained in his philosophy of history that man advances through the evolutionary stages of his development by conflict. We have a thesis of truth or half-truth at a given stage of development which is met by the antithesis of another half-truth. These challenge, influence, interpenetrate each other until, preserving the measure of value in each, man rises to a higher synthesis of truth in a new epoch. Marx believed that successive epochs of slavery, feudalism, capitalism and communism evolve by necessary, inexorable, economic laws until man reaches the final term, the highest stage of all, in the complete sharing of communism.

Without for a moment believing that history runs in such fixed and rigid channel beds as the over-simplified dogma of Marx maintained, we yet believe in the general principle of evolutionary development. When we review the glaring evils of the social injustice of capitalism as practiced in Europe and America, or those of communism with its denial of liberty as it actually operates in Russia, can we believe that either of these is the final term or the highest stage in man's evolutionary development? Must we be offered the bitter alternative of material prosperity, for some, at the price of social injustice, or of social justice at the cost of tyranny? Cannot a higher synthesis of the future achieve both freedom and social justice, both "liberty *and* union," individual initiative and social cooperation? Must we choose between the Scylla and Charybdis of unjust capitalism and tyrannical communism? Can we not steer a middle course avoiding the evils of both? Must we have the domination of the many by the few, whether of the fifty-eight men of wealth who are now said to "rule America," or the less than fifty-eight in the centralized group which dominates the hard "monolithic" communist world?

Russia has no monopoly of the ideal of justice, nor have Anglo-Saxon countries a monopoly of liberty. Let us note the advance of a country like Denmark. There we have no two simple classes of exploiters and exploited. The large estates have been divided up. Roughly, nine-tenths of the farmers own their own farms. Nine-tenths of them belong to their advanced and highly successful cooperatives. These cooperative societies are more efficient and prosperous than those of Russia, and they are not controlled by steam-roller methods. The farmers of Denmark are better off and better educated than those of Russia. They are not confined to the alternative of a *laissez faire* competitive capitalism or a dictatorship of communism. The world has other alternatives.

If it be said that Denmark is prevailingly rural we can turn to the British Labor Party or the Social Democratic Party of Germany or to many others. We find no call either to hold them up as models of attainment nor to pour forth scorn and hatred and misrepresentation concerning them as in Russia. We have come not to destroy but to fulfill. And we do not find any sudden, dazzling and final attainment either in capitalism or communism, in democracy or dictatorship. Panacea there is none. All social theories are on trial.

There are many times "seven thousand who have not bowed the knee" to the tyranny of either system and who refuse to be silent about the wrong of either, or the values of both. They hold their heritage of the ideal of liberty and democracy which they refuse to surrender even though it has never been fully realized. They too share in the passion for social justice and they demand and will work for nothing less than both ideals. They, as well as extreme capitalists or communists, have their aims, their programs and policies. And these are neither the greed of private profit for the few, nor the tyranny of a single class dictatorship for the many. Here are some of their objectives:

1. The protection of the workers by hand and brain against the four great risks of industry and indeed of life itself—accidents, illness, old age and unemployment. The United States is years behind most other civilized countries in the protection of its workers. The increasingly rapid changes in industry, leading to technological unemployment; the scrapping of men in middle age in our heavy industries, after ten or fifteen years of exhausting toil; the refusal of great numbers of corporations to employ new workers after reaching forty, forty-five or fifty years of age—these and other factors are leading to increasing insecurity as the years go on. Society, not the individual, should assume the burden, through various forms of social insurance of these risks which now bring so much tragedy into the life of tens of thousands of our people. Supplementing social insurance, we call for a long-range plan of public works in city, state and nation and a comprehensive system of public employment agencies.

2. The restoration of an increasing share in the wealth created by society to the community for social purposes, through the imposition of higher income and inheritance taxes on the higher income levels and of land values taxes.

Society should have at its disposal for health, for educational, for recreational and other public activities a far larger fund than it can now depend upon. Higher taxation would increase this fund and at the same time lessen the unjust inequalities of income which are vitiating our whole national life.

3. The reorganization under public ownership and operation of such strategic industries as are now being grossly mismanaged or which are gouging the public through excessive charges and the regulation of which has broken down. In the forefront of these two types of industrial undertakings come the chaotic coal industry, and the highly concentrated electric power industry. Domestic consumers in the cities of northern New York under private ownership have to pay two or three times as much for their electricity as do housewives in Ontario cities, where electricity is generated, transmitted and distributed by public agencies, while large power consumers pay from 60 to 170 per cent more in the New York centers and large commercial users pay from about 40 per cent to more than three times the costs for similar service in the Ontario cities.

4. The freeing of labor from unfair legal restrictions upon their activities which take such forms as yellow dog contracts, the virtual prohibition of boycotting and effective peaceful picketing, and the rigorous use of injunctions to hamper almost their every action. The very life blood of the labor movement beats through the channels by which it may organize and consolidate its group concerns. If these are choked, the labor movement cannot live; and the protec-

tion of labor in these essentials should be a first charge upon any party which honestly seeks to promote the basic interests of the laboring millions.

5. A program of farm relief which will reduce the disparity between urban and rural prices, not by giving a bonus to stimulate the export of food products and thus artificially increase the prices of agricultural goods, but by removing as rapidly as possible the high tariffs on manufactured goods. This will at once lower the prices of the goods which the farmer buys such as textiles, farm machinery and fertilizer. Moreover by permitting foreign countries to sell more manufactured goods to us, we will be able to sell more agricultural products such as cotton, wheat and pork to them. This will bring higher prices to farmers on their agricultural commodities and thus help in a double way to restore the balance between industry and agriculture which is so sorely needed. An agricultural program must also include far greater aid to cooperative effort than has hitherto been attempted.

6. The granting of fuller opportunity for development to the Negroes. The states should spend increasing sums to raise the level of Negro education, and Federal aid might appropriately be devoted to this purpose. Federal protection against lynching should also be accorded the Negro, and he should be given a fuller opportunity to function as a worker and as a citizen.

7. The freeing of Western civilization from the menace of another war. Unless the forces of destruction in the present nationalistic system are checked, the Western World

at best will be hurried into another far more disastrous war than that from which we emerged a decade ago. More concretely, they insist on withdrawal of the marines from Haiti and Nicaragua, the removal of financial and military dictatorships, sponsored by the citizens or government of the United States, from Latin American countries and the restoration of their national sovereignty; the carrying out of America's promise to restore Filipino independence; the radical reduction of naval and army forces and the government building of naval vessels under government auspices to the end of taking the profit out of armaments pending the day of complete disarmament; the recognition of the Russian Republic; the entrance of the United States into the League of Nations; and the organization of international economic commissions on raw materials, tariffs, investments, etc., in an attempt to minimize economic friction among various countries.

8. The reorganization of the judicial system of the country to the end that the courts may work more speedily, more justly, and with less autocracy than in the past. There is need also of a philosophy. Nor can this any longer be an individualistic, *laissez faire* philosophy, formulated to fit a primitive agricultural and handicraft civilization, and based on the false hypothesis that we are still living in the days of "rugged individualism." We are now living in the twentieth century, in the days of huge aggregations of people in crowded cities, of enormous private monopolies and combines. Only a philosophy of cooperation, of collectivism, of associated effort for the common good, is applicable to the

needs of the common people today. And this must be the social philosophy underlying the great future party of the masses.

The above eight points are quoted from the pamphlet *Why a Political Realignment?* by Professor Paul Douglas issued by the League for Independent Political Action.[1] They represent a very brief and partial statement of the aims and ideals of a growing number in America who despair of any fearless or adequate reforms from the political party of wealth and privilege, of high tariffs and political corruption in cities like Chicago and Philadelphia, or of the party of the reactionary solid South and Tammany Hall. Many are determined to build, as did Kier Hardy and Ramsay MacDonald in England, a third party in America that shall in time combine farmer, labor and intellectual elements, and that shall demand the eight points mentioned above and more—in a word both liberty and justice.

This earnest group is overawed or dismayed neither by the wealth, or power, or numbers or evils of capitalism or communism, or of the old political parties mentioned above. The members will doubtless be called "Reds supported by Moscow gold" in reactionary America, and sneered at as timid "reformist" compromisers by dogmatic communists. But they intend to pursue their ideal of a higher synthesis that shall combine individual liberty and social justice. To this synthesis both thesis and antithesis will contribute, both America and Russia will have their part to play.

[1] The League for Independent Political Action, 52 Vanderbilt Avenue, New York, John Dewey, Chairman; Howard Y. Williams, Executive Secretary.

The capitalist world will not remain stationary. The vast process of socialization is everywhere at work and widely manifest. The uniting of industry in trusts and ever larger units is only part of this process. Russia also is not stationary but is changing more rapidly than any country in the world. The vast work of education, not only in schools, but in cooperatives, trade unions, youth organizations and local self-government, will have an almost inevitable democratic trend in ever-widening circles. No tyranny can permanently maintain itself even in Moscow. Perhaps the gathering force of socialization on the one hand and of democratization on the other both make toward a final and higher synthesis.

If this be so, and if there be any philosophy of history, instead of one civilization possessing a monopoly of all the virtues assailed by a revolution that is a compound of all the vices, as we have seen we have in the world today two antithetic and challenging social orders as thesis and antithesis, neither of them perfect or final, which may both make their contribution to a higher stage or a final synthesis. If this be so, let us understand the important part America is destined to play, as well as the necessity for the reform of the evils which have been mentioned and of the vast process of socialization which must take place if she is to fulfill her destiny. Also, in spite of all the menace of a dictatorship, let us give full credit to the possible contribution of the Soviet Union. But whether it be good or evil we are unescapably confronted by *The Challenge of Russia*.

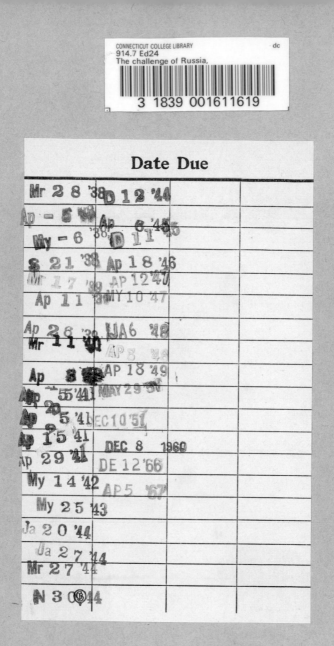

Date Due

Mr 28 '38	D 12 '44	
Ap - 5 '38	Ap 6 '45	
My - 6 '38	D 11 '45	
S 21 '38	Ap 18 '46	
Mr 17 '39	AP 12 '47	
Ap 11 '39	MY 10 47	
Ap 26 '39	JA 6 '48	
Mr 11 '40	AP 8 '48	
Ap 8 '40	AP 18 '49	
Ap 5 '41	MAY 29 '50	
Ap 5 '41	DEC 10 '51	
Ap 15 '41	DEC 8 1960	
Ap 29 '41	DE 12 '66	
My 14 '42	AP 5 '67	
My 25 '43		
Ja 20 '44		
Ja 27 '44		
Mr 27 '44		
N 30 '44		